# NAPLES

AGENTS IN AMERICA
THE MACMILLAN COMPANY
66 FIFTH AVENUE, NEW YORK

## PERGOLA

In the summer villa of Doctor Munthé, above Anacapri. The villa is built on the site of an old Roman
dwelling.

# : : : : NAPLES : : : :
## PAINTED BY AUGUSTINE FITZGERALD · DESCRIBED BY SYBIL FITZGERALD · PUBLISHED BY ADAM & CHARLES BLACK · LONDON

Published June 1904

# Preface

THESE pages, illustrated and written during a long summer round the Bay of Naples, are not only connected with the recollection of the country itself, but with the pleasant memory of many a kind suggestion and much help from Neapolitan friends whose names we mention here in grateful recognition,— Signora Mathilde Serao, Duca and Duchessa Dusmet de Smours, and Signor Salvatore di Giacomo. Many of the gardens painted in this book are also reminiscent of the kind hospitality and courtesy of their proprietors.

*May* 1904.

v

# Contents

vii

# Contents

## CHAPTER VIII

## CHAPTER IX

## CHAPTER X

## CHAPTER XI

## CHAPTER XII

# List of Illustrations

ix

# List of Illustrations

# List of Illustrations

# List of Illustrations

*The Illustrations in this volume have been engraved and printed by the
Carl Hentschel Colourtype Process.*

# NAPLES

## CHAPTER I

### NAPLES

"Où sont nés le maccaroni
Et la musique."

ALFRED DE MUSSET.

NAPLES and the province lying round it may be regarded as an epitome of Art and Nature. Here "winter is a word, and the commonest objects are as lovely as the rarest." Yet, in comparison with the mass of literature and art produced under the influence of Central Italy, little has been inspired by the South. There is, as it were, an invisible borderland across Italy, dividing the country loved by our modern poets, painters, and sculptors, from the land loved by the ancient Greeks. It is another world, and almost another race inhabit it. Its loveliness has grown with time into a proverb, and no longer inspires to song as of old. "The ideal of Nature exceeds that of man," wrote Hans Andersen years ago, when he found himself in this fairy world of his dreams. It is justly said that a visit to Italy has been the turning-point in many

I

lives, and certainly great careers of the last century bear
out the assertion. Since that golden age of poetry
when Shelley and Keats, Landor and the Brownings,
Ruskin and a whole world of gifted travellers, poured
into Italy, the North of Europe has felt a passionate
attraction towards the South. And if the intellectual
charm of Naples is more illusive than that of Rome or
of Florence, its beauty, at least, has no rival. There is
something in the soft and limpid loveliness of the Bay
of Naples that may well appeal to our Northern races
with the intensity of a passion. I do not mean to
include the life there—the life of the great, sordid
" Paris" of Italy, which, with its depths of poverty,
vice, and misery, lies like a great shadow in this world
of sunshine—but only speak of the natural scenery,
which embraces even these dark things with such tender-
ness. It is a beauty which the hand of man cannot
destroy. The midland sea is as blue, the curves of the
bay are as sweeping, as in the days when lovers of Nature
heard there the voices and the songs of their Gods.

To approach Naples to the best advantage, you must
go by sea. A wide view is before us of the headlands,
softened by distance, and of the harbour, which lies like
a great opal reflecting colours and sunshine as glowing
as those of the East, and yet far softer. There is something Homeric in the setting of this cluster of sea-washed
towns, extending in a wide half-circle from Posillipo
to Sorrento. In the near background rises the most
celebrated volcano in the world, purple Vesuvius, whose
ravelled cloud extends across the heavens. No longer

THE "GRIDONE," LEADING UP FROM
THE VIA CHIAIA

The popular flower market of Naples.

# Naples

does the luxuriant growth of the South clothe the summit
with the vineyards of long ago, when gardens crept up to
the very mouth of the crater, when mossy grass encircled
it as with a velvet belt, and the rose-coloured homes
of the inhabitants clustered round its knees as closely as
they had clustered in the thoughtless days of Pompeiian
splendour.  The molten lava upon its sides has taken
weird and fantastic shapes, which have been likened to a
confused mass of fallen horses and riders contorted upon
a field of battle.   One hardy flower still lingers there—

> " La qual null' altro allegra arbor nè fiore
>     Tuoi cespi solitari in torno spargi,
>     Odorata ginestra." [1]

So wrote the greatest of Italy's nineteenth-century poets
before the snowy cloud above the mountain had again
darkened to blood-red, and before again its fiery tongue
had licked away the persistent trace of vegetation.  Well
may the sleep of Vesuvius be likened to " some great
trance, the ages coming and going all the while."

The eruption of 1631 produced much Neapolitan
literature, poetical and scientific.  The following is a
free translation of one of the three somewhat over-
wrought poems on Vesuvius which were written at that
time by Gian Battista Basile, author of the *Pentamerone*,
whose works are now very rare :—

> " With strenuous throb of fire and mighty aim,
>     The earth is furrowed as by a monstrous plough ;

---

[1] " Where no other laughing tree or flower
        Encircles thy lonely growth,
        Perfumed genet."

3

# Naples

Gathered to its breast the fire seeds now
Gush forth in fervent rivers of liquid flame.
Thence to fertilise, the swift hours bear
Their amplitude of ashes to the shore
Where the Tyrrhenian sea receives once more
A wasted harvest of profound despair.
But, e'en though mortals suffer vital harm,
Great Vesuvius, exhausted in its turn,
Knows no relief for all those wounds that burn
Beneath the settling cinders, white and calm ;
Nor from the stupor of its fiery breath
Can rend apart Hell's images,—and Death."

The splendid harbour of Naples seems entitled by
Nature to be a greater shipping port than it is. But
the Neapolitan is often his own enemy, and, in spite
of the efforts of his country towards advance, is not
sufficiently lavish in his labour. He is content to live
on a crust of bread rather than better himself. Misery
in this blazing sunshine loses more than half its horrors,
and much of the pity given to the poor is wasted.
A lady told me that one day, while walking along the
shore, she saw a ragged and half-starved man lying
on the sand. Thinking that he would be only too
thankful to earn a few soldi, she asked him to carry
her box and camp-stool for her.

"Grazie, Signora, ma ho gia mangiato oggi," was
the answer.

Similarly, I have been told of an Italian baker who
happened to make a certain biscuit which gradually
became a kind of "Sally Lunn" in popularity among
the foreign residents. It brought him an increased

4

NAPLES, FROM THE PARCO GRIFEO

*clientèle*, and his fortune as a baker seemed assured ; but one fine day the delightful little cakes were not forthcoming, and why ?

"Alas, Signora, I had to cease making the dolci : so many ladies wanted them ! "

But poverty has brought out much that is sympathetic in the character of the Neapolitans. A great traveller, who had profoundly studied human nature in many parts of the world, said that if he were to find himself alone, starving, and without a penny, he would prefer of all places to find himself in the slums of Naples. So high an opinion had he formed of this apparently degraded but kindly people. One starving man will share his wretched meal of bread and an onion with another, and both will laugh and joke the while, as if it were a meal fit for a king. Misery never deadens their sense of life and amusement ; and so ungovernable is their love of pleasure, they will pawn or sell their last possession to go to a Festa. A woman will sell her bed to buy a worthy dress in which to appear at her daughter's wedding, or for a first communion ; and to bury their dead with pomp the people will resort to the last and most touching sacrifices. Their sense of honour is often as keen as ours, though different in kind—for the knife is ever ready to play a part in it. "They belong, indeed, to the country that uses the knife." Brothers will defend their sisters' virtue, and husbands their wives' good name, at the cost of their lives, and a wrong committed against their women is avenged to the death. Their natures are so passionate that only too easily does tragedy enter into their life ; but, fortunately or unfortunately, they soon forget. Unlike the Sicilians, the Neapolitan poor are a people without memories. If to-day be sunny, why remember that yesterday was dark with clouds ?

But, if they are among the most passionate of people, they are also the least sentimental, mixing up their love affairs and their money questions with an ingenuousness which would embarrass the most practical bourgeoisie of other countries. The young girl hastens to value her betrothal ring, so that she may purchase a gift in return of not more than a third of its value, that being considered sufficient. The deliberation with which gifts are made robs them of any poetry they might have, and the *dot* is even more openly discussed in Naples than in Paris. The feeling for money is a very curious study here, and it is sometimes hard to detect how far it is purely practical. To hide the lack of it, or to indulge the love of show, the poor people have recourse to absurd measures. The wedding presents are often merely lent for the occasion ; perhaps even the jewels are hired from shops. At one time families owned carriage doors painted with their arms, which were fitted into hired vehicles. In one of the Neapolitan dialect plays, one of the characters is made to say,

"Take away my honour, but leave me my purse ! "

Whether or not this expresses the sentiment of certain classes in Naples, all I can say is that the people seem

6

# Naples

to me remarkably generous, and generosity among the poor is proverbial.

Out of his own country, and far from the corrupt influence of the Camorra, which undermines energy and independence, the Neapolitan is a hard-working man. In every country in the world he may be traced, and no great works are ever completed to which Italian labour does not contribute. But out of their country, as in it, the Italian labourer is always underpaid. Because he can manage to subsist on cheaper food and less meat than the workman of another land, he is obliged to gain less in proportion. The injustice of such treatment is obvious. Abstinence from drink has never lessened a man's wages in England or else-where; but the Italian labourer must pay for his frugality.

The last time we visited Naples we decided to put up at Bertolini's new Palace Hotel, which is on the highest point, overlooking the whole town. For charm of position it is perhaps unique in all Europe. The rocky height on which it stands has been tunnelled by the shaft of a lift which carries its visitors up through the solid rock into the hotel itself, hundreds of feet above—a remarkable feat of engineering. The drive rapidly takes us out of the teeming and breath-less town—out of streets which might have been laid, for all the modern comfort they provide, with the clumsy stones which paved Pompeii. Leaving on our right the eccentric grey castle which has lately sprung upon the amazed eyes of all who know Naples, from

the solid rock, we follow a winding road towards the
Parco Griffeo, passing by the private gardens of many
villas into which we can just glimpse.    They are
filled with aloes, acacia trees, palms, and roses; wild
geraniums bloom on the road.    From the terrace of
the hotel a splendid panorama is at our feet.    The
great sordid city, encircled by its five castles, lies half-
hidden from our view.    Far away the white and rose-
tinted villas of Posillipo glitter in the sun, and almost
lost in the blue haze of the sea lie the dream-like islands
of Ischia and Capri.    I know not what there is in the lines
of the headlands and the contours of the islands that
continually reminds one of the great Greek wanderer.

Above the hotel on the Vomero is situated the
beautiful Villa Floridiana, presented by Ferdinand I.
to Lucia Migliaccio, a Sicilian widow.    A beautiful,
and, I believe, unique, miniature of this lady is seen in
the Filangieri Museum, in which she is represented
wearing a red turban and sash, with a face pensively
gentle.    Ferdinand must have had a strong infatuation
for her.    She was over forty when he married her,
clandestinely, and the funeral services for his dead
Queen were still going on in the churches.    Perhaps
he was glad at last to have a wife genuinely feminine,
and not, as his former spouse had been, "il suolo uomo
del regno di Napoli."

The villa was fitted up with most extravagant
luxury.    It possessed a theatre, a coffee-house, even a
tiny temple; the whole of the grounds were alive with
birds, among them swans and pheasants, while deer and

even wild animals filled the park. This exotic character has, of course, vanished, and the beautiful villa is now the property of a foreigner. The view from the terrace, like all the views from the Vomero, has something singularly tranquil in it, and it is a spot which has ever been peculiarly attractive to Neapolitans.

Near the Floridiana, and once a part of it, stands the pretty Villa Lucia, which, like so many bits of the Parco Griffeo, has passed into private hands. It is said to have changed hands on one occasion because the wife of the owner wearied of having " une cuvette bleu " eternally under her eyes. In its garden may still be seen the marble fountain with an allegorical group composed of a figure poising a garland on Love. Through the hole of the garland the sun-ray passes, and marks constantly the date of the marriage of the king and the Floridia.

Here, far above the town itself, the air is decidedly purer than on the sea-shore, and the breeze is exquisitely scented. In the evening the view is surpassingly beautiful. To the west is the afterglow of the sunset, and the light of the rising moon spreads a silver halo round the crest of Vesuvius, where a red glow of flame throbs from time to time towards the sky. The city below is like a vast sea of electric stars. Here is one shooting down the hill, and passing away beneath us—the electric tram which follows the curve of the Corso. Beyond lies the dark sea upon which the moonlight will soon be trembling.

# Naples

"O, balmy nights of Naples! is it but wayward indulgence,
If for a few swift moments the revelling heart is oblivious
For thy fair sake of St. Peter, of e'en the divine Pantheon,
Ay, and of Monte Mario?   And thou, O Villa Pamphili,
E'en thy fountains of crystal, thy laurel-dimmed paths are
forgotten."[1]

But for those who wish to study the life and ways
of the people the Corso is too far away from the town,
and too far from the picturesque life of the fishermen,
who are a great feature of Naples, and of all the little
fishing towns along the shore.   Crowds of idlers, leaning over the sea wall, seem never weary of watching
the hauling in of the nets, which are very large and
stretch far out to sea.   Sometimes as many as twenty
men will be hauling the same rope, and the operation
seems to go on for hours; but I myself have never
"been in at the finish."   If interested, the loiterers
looking on will often lend a hand, and the scene is
full of animation.   These fishermen are as dark as the
Pompeiian bronzes in their Naples Museum, and a
breath of the sculpturesque spirit of antiquity seems
to touch us in looking at them.   But the genius such
forms once inspired seems asleep.   The artistic character of a race undergoes changes as inexplicable as
its political development.   "O, com' è bello!" says
the poorest peasant before any beautiful object, and no
doubt the sense of beauty is as alert in these southern
races as in the Græco-Roman workmen of the Roman
Empire.   But the sacred fire of creative enthusiasm is

[1] Translated from the German of Von Platen.

WOMAN KNITTING, NEAPOLITAN TYPE

extinguished. The tradition of the past overshadows the production of the present.

The unity of Italy has given her youth only in name and in political combinations ; but her traditions, social and artistic, seem to fetter her to the past, and are more of an obstacle than an assistance to her progress. At least, this is the impression strongly borne in upon one from personal contact with the artists of the country and the representatives of its social life. Thus, a country follows mysteriously a law of evolution, the secret of which has always defied the critic of art as well as the historian.

The word " decadence," which is generally used to cover the period of a decline in art, is here inadequate. We have only to turn into the Museum of Naples to discover *chef d'œuvres* of sculpture which were produced in the distinctly decadent age of the Roman Empire. In Italy there is now a distinct national advance in which the commercial conditions of the country are steadily improving, while science is flourishing and education becoming more general ; yet this period is almost sterile of artistic production. Morelli may be named as a true and great exception ; but he stands alone. An admirer of the " genie de la race Latine " can scarcely believe in its ultimate extinction. But it is a curious fact that the glorious days of Greek and Roman art (as of still more ancient periods) were days of slavery ; and one is tempted to ask whether times of comparative liberty have not proved its death-warrant. Be this as it may, we must not forget that in the south of Italy

languor and weakness of morale go hand in hand with
acuteness and intellectual activity. The lower as well
as the upper classes are naturally intelligent; and
while the north of Italy is superior in moral qualities
and steadiness, the Neapolitans are, by dint of their
intelligence, and perhaps unscrupulousness, making themselves a strong political factor in modern Italy.

Crispi may be taken as the most brilliant type of what
the South Italian may rise to. In spite of the attacks
of many enemies, and in spite of his latter-day un-
popularity, he was for many years not only the strongest
statesman in Italy, but he succeeded in voicing the
Nationalist aspirations of his whole country. Had he
kept up with the times more resolutely, his power might
have been far greater. But his ideas (to quote from
one who knew him intimately) remained at the same
point for the last twenty years of his life. In his conversation it was remarked that the names of the younger
generation, however brilliant and promising, were passed
over, while those of the compatriots of his own youth
were continually on his lips. As though fossilised in
his prime, Crispi remained a great man; but he grew
no greater.

This influence of the South in politics is viewed with
disfavour by the central Italians. They feel, with a
certain justice, that the country, unified by the minds
and the robust integrity of Cavour, Mazzini, Minghetti,
and the other great leaders of the Risorgimento, is
falling under the influence and the corruption of the
South. Hence I have noticed an intense acrimony

towards the Neapolitan in the minds of many of the Piedmontese and Tuscans, an acrimony which is returned with interest. The unity of Italy does not seem to have amalgamated the races of the North and South any more than has been the case in Austria-Hungary.

This supports the assertion that the moral slackness of the South does not go hand in hand with intellectual decay.

The Neapolitan is said to be able to conquer the difficulties of reading and writing in three months! Taine, in his critical work on Naples, says : "Il n'y a pas de race plus fine, plus prompte à saisir et à deviner toutes les idées. Le paysan, enrichi et éclairé, deviendra plus libéral." These words were written before the unity of Italy. The Camorra itself is an extraordinary instance of misdirected intelligence. How any brain can control the countless threads of intrigue in this society is a mystery. The ramifications of this body completely undermine the foundations of law and order, and have made an effective secret-service system under the ostensible régime of justice and municipal government. Not very long ago the tourist season in Naples was threatened by rumours of several cases of plague in the town. As a matter of fact, there was no truth in the report. Being for the moment in need of funds, the Camorra endeavoured to levy blackmail on the hotel-keepers ; but they met with a decided refusal. A few days afterwards the newspapers were filled with reports of an outbreak of plague, much to the damage of the hotels. Is it not curious that a large proportion of the governing intellect of Italy should have its origin in a town where such a condition of corruption exists? But secret societies have always played a great part in Italian history, and no doubt always will.

The stranger would hardly guess at these facts, which lie hidden beneath a smiling surface, beneath the volatile and buoyant spirit of the inhabitants. And herein, perhaps, we have the real charm of Naples! In its vivid contrast of light and shade, of misery and well-being, of languor and buoyancy, there is the continual triumph of the sun over the shadow,—in appearance at all events. The Sun God seems ever transfixing the serpent with his glittering shafts, and the luxuriant beauty of this land spreads a golden veil over the misery of its inhabitants.

> " O Natura cortese,
>     Son questi i doni tuoi,
>     Questi i deletti sono
>     Che tu porgi ai mortali."[1]

Here where the leaves of the trees laugh and gentle breezes whisper through their branches, the drowsy toiler in the sun seems half unburdened of his care.

In Naples the same changes which have transformed Milan, and are transforming Florence, are at work. All artists must deplore them, for they mean the supplanting of the old and picturesque by the purely useful and banal. Where once narrow houses with roof-

---

[1] " O, gracious nature,
    These are thy gifts,
    These are the delights,
    That thou givest to mortals."

PORTO CAPUANA, NAPLES

One of the old gates of the town.

gardens, jutting corners, and quaintly constructed arches and stairs, broke the line of the narrow streets, are now seen rows of high modern buildings. Electric trams run through the streets, and much of the local colour is gradually retreating to the older quarters of the town. In the last ten years this inevitable change has been creeping into all the smaller towns from Naples to Castellamare. Soon there will be a tramway along one of the most beautiful drives in the world—from Castellamare to Sorrento.

Hand in hand with progress we find curiously obsolete customs. In hired vehicles the horses are not driven with a bit. A small bar is fixed over the nose, and the rein is attached to it. This custom, however provincial it may appear, seems to give excellent results. The horse is quite under the control of the driver, and can drink with ease. I have often asked myself whether this primitive system may not have some advantage.

The natives' general love of display is vividly seen in the trappings of their horses. What must be intended as an ornament, a thing like an enormous duster, is attached to the animal's head. The tinkling of many bells relieves the monotony of the poor beast's life, and the cracking of whips no doubt relieves it more. The decoration of the mules is still yet more bizarre. On the back of the animal—and again for apparently decorative effect,—rises an enormous brass column, surmounted by a tuft of fur and adorned with brass nails. Between the ears and over the nose hangs a mass of soft light fur and red tassels. I know of no instance in

which so much unnecessary trouble has been taken for
artistic effect. To see a long line of mules passing
along the white and dusty roads, tinkling with many
bells and gay with this fantastic blazonry, is to fancy
oneself in the days of the Mamelukes—such a touch of
Eastern magnificence is in the simple scene. The mules
pass us, not only with the jingling of bells, but also with
the drivers' snatches of light-hearted song, the gay songs
of Piedigrotta. It seems as if these popular canzonetti
were a key to the people's character. Every year a
competition is held for them at the *fête* of the Madonna
of Piedigrotta, and a prize awarded to the most successful composer. Imagine this scene on a starlit autumn
night, the sea bright as polished crystal. Not a single
cloud is in the sky, save that beautiful column rising like a
stone pine above Vesuvius. The city and all around the
bay is a glitter of lights. On the roads, white with dust,
not less than some twenty thousand gaily-dressed men,
women, and children are moving along, tired, overheated,
but light-heartedly happy. It is the night of their
greatest Festa, a festa which will last with song and
dance far into the cool morning hours! Over this mass
of human beings, with their dark and laughing faces,
play the coloured lights which the boys carry and wave
about on long sticks. Other lads carry poles garlanded
with delicious fruit and gay with paper flowers. Sometimes the light gleams on the bright copper boilers which
men bear cleverly poised in baskets on their heads : the
vessels hold that great delicacy for the poor—snail soup !
Along the sides of the road, especially round the Grand

Hotel, are piled small mountains of water melons and Indian figs. It is a wonderful scene, and almost terrific is the noise! Thousands of men and boys are playing on their curious musical instruments,—tin trumpets, wooden hammers, and large shells—which produce a strange booming roar. And stranger still is the instrument called the *putipù*, which gives an almost unearthly sound. This consists of an open terra-cotta jar, with sheep skin tightened over it, and a hole drilled in the skin, through which a stick is worked up and down. Where could this instrument have originated, if not in the East?

At midnight begins the procession of decorated carts full of dressed-up men and women. One by one these carts pause, and the occupants in turn sing their new Piedigrotta songs. The seething crowds listen critically, approving or condemning; and early in the morning, while yet the stars are in the sky, the prizes are awarded to the composers whose songs have been adjudged the best.

Song and dance must be heard and seen together to be fully appreciated. The blue sky must be overhead; the radiant sea must be in the background; the faces of the singers must be olive-tinted and dark-eyed! Alas, the real tarantella dance-music and song are becoming spoiled by the critical taste of foreigners, who too often judge by the musical standard of their own countries. Could they be superseded by a higher music, this would not be so regrettable; but a bird's note cannot be changed, and in these Piedigrotta songs

3      

a delicate national vein is heard, which, becoming extinct, would be followed by nothing but imitations from other countries. For long past there has existed here in the South a school of song which is quite unique ; into it any introduction of orchestration is fatal. The mandolin, the guitar, the castanets,—these are their natural instruments ; and, strange as it may seem to critics, the rich and untrained voice, when accompanied only by these simple instruments, has a wild charm of its own, quickly lost in the midst of a more complicated orchestra. The violin, badly or indifferently played, has done more to destroy the charm of the native melodies than anything I know of.

The music and songs of the tarantella are rarely heard in Naples now, save by visitors at the hotels. Absurd bands of men and women, overdressed, and with exasperatingly sharp voices, still entertain them of an evening. But listening to noisy stamping on parquet floors in overheated rooms, hearing the native songs accompanied by the town orchestra, is highly ridiculous. Only at Sorrento the tarantella still keeps something of its old charm. Of an evening the dancers take their places in the open courtyard of the hotel. Their background is a garden of orange and lemon trees and flowers, the breath of which perfumes the air deliciously. The stars twinkle in the dark blue sky, and the whole scene is lovely and poetical. The women are dressed in bright costumes of red and green, with white muslin aprons. Beads of glass are round their necks ; gold and coral gleam in their ears. The figures are

A SINGER IN THE TARANTELLA

glittering in a semi-obscurity as they move against the dark trees. The castanets resound in the air, and we are carried away by the laughing music. A distinctly humorous element crops out in many of the songs, written, of course, in dialect. In one the braying (and even the kicking) of the ass is imitated with drollery ; in others a sadder and more plaintive note is struck, reminding one forcibly of the far-off, Arab origin of all the dances, which spread from Spain to Italy hundreds of years ago. Never do we hear the cheaply sentimental note ; and as to the comic songs, although coarse and often full of double meanings, they have not the common vulgarity of our music-halls. Happily, the songs that are born among the people in any country, songs which are national in their origin, are always free from this element of our modern civilisation.

# CHAPTER II

NAPLES—THE MUSEUM—CAPO DI MONTE

I REMEMBER well the first time we walked through the Toledo. It was a beautiful day early in the spring. Wishing to see something of the life of the people, we had lunched at Gambrinus, a really characteristic restaurant in the very heart of the town. Though not frequented by the *beau monde* of Naples, it is full of local colour. The walls are panelled with paintings by Neapolitan artists, boldly painted in, and some full of merit. In all are seen the charming tints of landscape and figure in Capri and Sorrento. We took a small table close to the window—somewhat to our sorrow, for many hungry little faces looked in at us all through the meal. We ordered the typical Neapolitan *menu*, which is always ready. First came the historic macaroni, here called " pasta," on which the people seem almost wholly nourished, though in the days of Boccaccio and Petrarch it was an amusing novelty. This was followed by a plat of " fritto mista," which looks and tastes delicious. What it is made of only the Neapolitan knows, and he will not tell. Who shall say of this dish, when found

20

in the smaller cafés, whether it be cat, or dog, or rabbit ? All I know is that dogs have a mysterious way of disappearing hereabouts : the secret you must ask of the Camorra. A friend of ours, possessor of a valuable dog, and aware of this peculiarity, determined to take the matter courageously into his own hands. Fortunately, he knew the "Capo," the President, of this strange society, and went to him for assistance.

"I have," he said, "a beautiful dog, to whom I am devoted. When I walk about the streets of Naples I have to keep him always on the chain and literally never take my eyes off him. May I appeal to your kindness to assure me of the animal's safety ? "

He was listened to kindly. A careful note was taken of the dog's appearance and of its owner's address.

"You need have no further anxiety," said this quaint official of the underground world of Naples. And our friend now walks light-heartedly through the crowded streets of the town, and the dog runs wherever he pleases in safety.

But this is a digression. A fiasco of the light wine of Capri is before us sparkling in the mid-day sun : we are in the land of Bacchus, the natural garden of vineyards. These wines are too strong for foreigners like ourselves, and must be diluted with water. Many varieties bear soft Italian names—Vesuvio, Falerno, Lacrima Cristi, and so on.

After luncheon we wandered into the Toledo. Few of the foreigners walk in this street : the shops of tortoise-shell, of lace, or of coral, which most attract them, are found nearer the sea-front. On this lovely spring day the whole of the Neapolitan world seemed out-of-doors. Such a day the Italian loves—when the sun is not yet too hot and the deep shadows have lost the chill of winter.

> "How little they care,
>   While the weather holds fair,
>   What Europe may do with to-day."

The street is full of open fiacres, and in and out from under the very wheels run the flower-sellers with their large bouquets of stiffly-wired spring blossoms. These they toss into the carriages, and adroitly catch again if pitched out by irritated occupants. The drivers have the greatest difficulty in keeping off the small street arabs who cling to the backs of the vehicles, and in steering a course through the foot passengers, who walk anywhere rather than on the narrow pavements. The noise of the cracking whips and rattling of wheels over the uneven pavements is so uniformly deafening that one ceases to remark it.

There is a natural love and need of bright colour in this people. The soft tones that harmonise with our northern climate would appear faded against their brilliant sky. Their background is as often blue and gold as ours is grey. The poor women wear gaudy handkerchiefs around their necks ; the bodice and the skirt are invariably of different tints. The well-to-do also are fond of showy effect. Indeed, the Neapolitan

## ON THE MARINA, NAPLES

A drink and lemon booth. The vendors drive a
brisk trade all the year round. The older booths
were made of painted wood, but are now being
replaced by more elaborate ones of polished marble.

women have a style of dress distinctly different from that of Central Italy. The large picture hats are never out of fashion, any more than the little dark curls worn on either side of the olive-tinted brow. They prefer light colours as decidedly as the Roman lady prefers black. I have known soberly dressed Englishwomen who, after a few years' stay in Naples, have adopted colours that would dismay their oldest and dearest friends at home !

Now and then through the street crowd bearded monks pass us with arms folded under wide sleeves. Sometimes we pass a lemon stand, hung with fresh branches of mandarins and oranges and laden with glittering cans of iced water. Round it stands a group of thirsty men and boys. The Neapolitans are feverish in blood, and the harsh wine of their country does not slacken their thirst as do the cool fruit drinks.

At every step we are pursued by beggars—men, women, and children. I remember an English tourist who, in exasperation, mustered up all the Italian he knew, and, turning upon his tormentors, exclaimed loudly, "Vado, vado, a Diavolo!" This had a re-markable effect upon the superstitious people. Instead of having said what he had intended,—which, no doubt, the reader can divine,—he had angrily stated his intention of going to His Satanic Majesty himself.

Occasionally, in and out among the crowd, we recognise the unmistakable gait of a sailor, which reminds us that we are in a great seaport town, and that men-of-war are anchored in the harbour. Indeed,

not far off, near Castellamare, is one of the centres of
naval construction, where frequently is seen a half-built
leviathan in the slips.

The Toledo seems a street without an end.   Let
us branch off to the left and follow people into one of
the larger churches.   There are few beautiful and
historic interiors, as in Rome or Florence ; but they
are interesting to those who would study another side
of Neapolitan character—the devotional.   Take a chair
and sit quietly in the shade of a column, and you may
watch the poor steal in to some familiar place before
a shrine, and, after murmuring a few prayers, take up
their burden and go silently away.   One man, who
has knelt devoutly before the little Altar laden with
gilt and gauze flowers, will go out and needlessly lash
his cart-horse.   Another, perhaps a member of the
Camorra, will leave the confessional and commit some
petty theft.   The woman who looks up at the effigy
of the Holy Child may lately have deserted her own
infant, as is so common among the poor women of
Naples.   Their religion is poetry, not doctrine.   They
are intelligent, but not reflective.   Their ideas of eternal
punishment and reward are almost medieval, and in
their imagination the terrors of religion play a greater
part than the ethical teachings.   Their sensibility to
such impressions may be illustrated by a story culled
from a Neapolitan newspaper the other day.   A priest,
wishing to work upon his impressionable congregation
during a sermon upon future punishment, filled the
hidden parts of the church with men who groaned in

DANCER OF THE TARANTELLA AT
SORRENTO

anguish and rattled chains at appropriate points. This proved too much for the listeners. The experiment succeeded too well. They rushed in terror from the sacred precincts in a frenzy of religious fear, and many were injured in the panic which ensued. Inquiry brought the truth to light, and disgrace fell upon the too zealous Padre.

The first time I went into a church near Naples I noticed a coffin in the middle aisle with wreaths of flowers and lighted candles round it. Approaching, I saw, to my amazement, that the coffin was unclosed, and that the waxen face of a dead man was in full view. The sight of Death is far more impressive than the mere knowledge that Death is there, and perhaps it was for this reason that the people were allowed to wander in and receive into their impressionable natures the full meaning of " memento mori." Fewer men than women are seen in the churches,—as, indeed, is the case elsewhere in Italy. Among the younger generation and the student class free-thinking is not uncommon.

Let us say a few words about the University of Naples, one of the three important " accademie " which were the outcome of the intellectual movement of the Renaissance. This University makes the town a centre of learning as well as one of mere pleasure. Perhaps few of the travellers who pass through the throngs of careless idlers in the Toledo, or of the indolent pleasure-seekers in the Corso, realise that over a thousand students are working in their midst, that foreign men of learning

and science are engaged in lecture rooms and labora-
tories, and that there is here one of the most important institutions for zoological study. Such, however,
is the case. Naples is a cradle of scientific research.
What a gorgeous environment of Nature and Art!
Yet much of this is lost on the youth of the South.
Intense consciousness of the beauty and historic sentiment
of the South is a trait, rather, of our northern nature.
Such books as Hans Andersen's *Improvisatore* and
Lamartine's *Gaaziella* are the creations of northern
races. One seeks in vain in current Italian literature
for the charming appreciations of Savage Landor or for
such exquisite descriptions as Symonds and Ruskin
have given us. Italians themselves assert that no writer
has described the beauty of Italy as perfectly as
d' Annunzio ; but a study of his superb imagery shows
the influence of the North underlying it—the influence
of that English school which has made a poetry of the
" word-painting " of landscape and architecture. To
the rising generation of students this poverty in their
modern literature means little. Beauty is all around
them, and is too intimate a part of their life to require
a language. All that the University student asks is
that life be cheap and enjoyable. He realises the
beauty of his native land only when far from it, and
homesick, with a homesickness which is said to surpass
that of other countries.

Imagine the days of vacation that can be passed at
Capri and Ischia, or at Rome, which lies so near !
Soon, it is said, an electric railway, which will rivet

LEMONADE-SELLERS OF NAPLES

still more closely these great cities, is to be made. A
new road, geographically shorter than the present one,
and reducing the six-hours' distance to three, is being
surveyed. This is a subject for the enthusiasm of the
youth of Naples, and who shall say that such enthusiasm
is misplaced ? It is the Italian's strength that he is all
for modern movement and advance—for the "time of
day," as our Cockneys at home would say. Surrounded
though he is by so much that is behind the times, his
ideal is for the latest invention, the fastest train, the
newest methods of science. The magnificent ruins in
which he was born pass unnoticed. His aspirations are
those of a young people growing as rapidly as children
grow amid the relics and the mouldering loveliness of a
past which has no voice for them.

> "Above the graves of buried men
> The grass hath leave to grow";

and often does it strike one, when wandering in the
South, with what determined hopefulness new homes,
new centres, new and flourishing vineyards, have sprung
up over the ruins of buried towns. Talk to the Italian
of progress in any form, but not of the poetry and fetters
of long ago, not of the vanished glories of Paestum
and Girgenti,—these find no response. But eagerly
will he discuss the material advancement of his country
—its rapid train service and its commercial prosperity.
To him life is the more vital since it has come so late ;
strides must be taken where others walk. So there is
no time to pause, to look back and to dream. We

have, it is true, one dreamy friend, who is continually searching for what he calls the " Soul " of the Italian people ; but such a mood must be explained by his over-study of the Pre-Raphaelite period. Is it possible that the Soul itself be Pre-Raphaelite ? At all events, we may say, with the celebrated ecclesiastic, that here, as in the country of his missions, all save the spirit of man is divine.

There is in the spring weather a softness which fills the heart with a great craving for I-know-not-what Pantheistic ideal. When day by day passes with perfection of warmth and sunlight, when the breezes gently stir the blue expanse of sea and sky, when a light violet mist softens the outlines of Ischia and Capri, we seem almost forced to turn to the days of Paganism, when each glade, each rivulet, had a soul embodied in a deity.

But the reader must not suppose, from these remarks made on a lovely day, that the climate here is a continual blaze of sunshine. Unfortunately this is not the case. In spring and autumn there are two seasons of heavy rain. And how entirely all is changed in Naples on a rainy day ! The streets that looked so gay in the sun, or were bathed in luminous shadow, become uniformly grey. Even Vesuvius is shrouded in mist, and the damp cold seems by contrast far more intense than it really is. Soon the streets are deserted, for the Neapolitan does not love rain—or, perhaps, water in any form. To the tourist this weather is extremely trying. At home he is independent of it ;

but hotel life in bad weather is depressing. At a moment like this we cannot do better than stroll through the great Museum. We must take one of the light carriages, and be jolted over the unspeakable pavement ; but we leave the sordid and chilling realities of outdoor life behind us when we penetrate to the glorious vision of antiquity within its walls.

A general survey of this Museum gives an impression distinctly different from that given by any other in the world. It is the only collection I know of in which the Gods of Greece and of Rome seem really to hover about their effigies. A mysterious paganism pervades the atmosphere. All seems real, vital, present, —not locked away in the lumber rooms of the past, as is so often felt elsewhere. Perhaps the nearness of origin has something to do with this sensation ; perhaps the surrounding landscape has attuned the mind to a closer grasp. However this may be, I think that every lover of Greek and Roman poetry will agree in recognising a subtle and indefinable charm in this beautiful collection. Great marble Gods gaze placidly at us, as though only spellbound and waiting for the touch of some Pygmalion to breathe again and to speak. One is quickly lost in reverie, and can almost fancy that ambrosial perfumes have penetrated through the grimy walls. What majestic repose is in the quiet limbs of these Gods and Goddesses, and what an antithesis to the restless turmoil and hurry of our own day ! May not this explain how the real secret of sculpture has been lost ? How can an age like our own—with its railways, telephones, and

*13334*

motor-cars—find an embodiment in an art which is the perfection of magnificent calm ?

Turn to Psyche with the divine intellectual brow. Of what does she dream? The eyes speak of profound dreamland ; the head, delicately poised on exquisite shoulders, seems to embody the most perfect blending in marble of physical and psychical beauty. She has well been named Psyche,—for it is indeed the statue of a soul, and no sculptor may hope to go further.

I love the wild and twisted forms of the fauns, with heads garlanded in berries and vines. One of them holds a lovely laughing child astride upon his shoulders. The position is the same as that in which children are held to-day in the East. The faun, stepping lightly, clashes cymbals in each hand, and, turning his head, greets the child's delighted eye with a smile. It is a smile in which may be read the whole genesis of the myths of the woodlands and the streams. Indeed, thronging memories of the singers of the woods and the waters awake in us before many of these marble groups. To what poet in chief shall we attribute our associations? Is it Theocritus, the "singer of the field and fold," the bard whose sweet words are fresh with the air of the sunny slopes of Sicily, the wild-cactus leaves, and the goats feeding from them? Or may it be, perhaps, the majestic echoes of Pindar that touch us when standing before the form of a hero or athlete whose limbs seem still to tremble from the glory of some Olympian contest? Perhaps, after all, it is to our Homeric memories that we owe the most. Every statue seems to be in one sense or another Homeric—in its simplicity or in its fibre. In all this art there is something epic.

And what glories of more recent art! Pass among the bronzes of those so-called decadent days. Here the achievement of a perfected artistic ideal is evident, and how little do these bronzes, full of fiery force, reflect the spirit of decline! Here the religious ideal is no more found: it has given place to forms realistic and grotesque in their powerful characterisation of Nature. A dwarfed and knotted Silenus staggers under the weight of a candelabra which he holds in his right arm. The muscles of his diminutive stature are strained and tense in a masterpiece of natural poise. A drunken faun reels backward, balancing an enormous wine-skin, his face a play of tipsy joviality. We can almost see the sunshine warm upon the figure, and the sense of movement fills it with breath. I know not what delicate psychology of spirit has enabled the creators of these types to extract from such simple material such perfect artistic achievement. These art treasures may be classed in the same category as the priceless gems of antiquity, where in a minute cameo colossal effects are produced, and breadth of treatment is tempered by exquisite refinement of proportion. And in these bronzes now before us there is an acute realism as modern as that which artists seek for in our own day, and with it a technical excellence which perhaps will never be surpassed.

So, in this epitome of antiquity in the Naples

31

Museum, we have passed through the whole scale of possible performance in sculpture—from echoes of stone-bound almost Egyptian Gods of the awakening days of Greek art, to the hyper-refined conceits of a period when " l'art pour l'art " had placed the sculptor on the throne and the shrine of his art in the erewhile temple of the Gods.

These bronzes lead us insensibly from thoughts on art and religion to the details in the daily life of the Pompeiians. Here are a hundred-and-one utensils and objects of decoration that ministered to their common wants and pleasures. Far away in the past, they yet seem near to us as we recognise so many familiar objects similar to those used in our daily life. Here are the mirrors and the little toilette articles that the ladies used in their boudoirs—

> " Dear dead women, with such hair too,
> What's become of all the gold
> Used to hang and brush their bosoms ? "

The jewels they wore are laid away in the glass cases, much as they may have been laid away in their wearers' jewel boxes. The little lamps that lighted their apartments still swing from the branching candelabra. The money box, the tiny Gods, the lares and penates of their long-extinguished hearths, the amulet, the talisman, the cineric urn,—all these details are gathered together and affect us strangely. Perhaps the most pathetic are the toys of the children, reminding us of the eternal springtime of life—the child life which is always growing out of death.

VEGETABLE SHOP, NAPLES

# Naples—The Museum—Capo di Monte

From the pictures on their walls we know that love
played a great part in this degenerate age. A sort
of troubadour element of song and dance is seen in
many of them. But of the love affairs of the ladies of
the Roman Empire we know nothing. No realistic
novel has come down to us, no intimate history of
their lives. The correct and lifeless inventions of
Becker's *Gallus* and *Charicles* cannot revive them.
The beautiful and languid forms of Alma-Tadema's
historic intellect are but fancies. All that belonged
to them we have—their horses' bits and harness,
the worn chariot-wheel, the mosaics upon which they
walked, even the loaves discovered intact in the baker's
tiny "boutique." But the secret of their lives is lost.

Bulwer's *Last Days of Pompeii* has always been a
favourite book of mine. The characters are vital and
human, and in it the lifeless streets of Pompeii seem again
to be filled with a pleasure-loving throng. Bulwer
has given us a picture of a fashionable watering-place
of the ancients, when the wealthy citizen of Rome vied
with his neighbour in the luxury of his habits and in the
critical delicacy of his taste. The sentiment of the
dialogue, the pathos of the romantic situations, are real
and human, and no other attempt, however scholarly,
has brought the dead past so vividly before us. But
to those who care to search for it there is more of the
breath of life in this collection of intimate objects in the
Museum rooms than in the pages of any modern writer
of romance or history. The art which man produces
every day is a mirror in which he himself is reflected—

his strength, his aspirations, and his limitations. As has been eloquently pointed out by Ruskin and Morris, the real history of man in any period is written by himself in what his own hands have made, and not in the records of governments and dynasties.

On leaving these beautiful relics a last thought strikes us of the keen sense of beauty of that period, and the buoyant enjoyment of life of which we have lost the secret. Wealth no longer gives us all we want, and does a sunny climate as often make us gay?

In a country so endowed by all the loveliness of Nature, where colour is so rich, and the life of the people is naturally so free and artistic, one might have supposed that in the palmy days of Italian painting a great school, comparable to that of Venice, might have flourished here. Such was not the case. To what extent political conditions affected art at Naples at that time—that is too intricate a question to discuss here. Let us see, at all events, what time has saved from the wreck of other schools in this Museum. It is, indeed, a curious jumble, this collection of pictures! In the eyes of the cicerone of Italy it has little value, since it contains few works of the highest order, and much that is spurious or of doubtful authorship. A veritable collection of odds and ends, drift-wood from the great centuries, when even obscure and nameless work has a fine savour of its own for the lover of painting and antiquity. The mere amateur will find little to interest him; but there are wonderful pearls among the débris.

Take, for example, Guido Reni's "Atalanta's Race."

# Naples—The Museum—Capo di Monte

Rarely have I seen any mention made of this masterpiece of the once popular and admired but now somewhat abused old master. This beautiful painting seems a sort of dream picture of the beauties of the Gods we have just been surveying—of their beauty as it might have existed in some great mural decoration in Rome or Pompeii, destroyed ere it reached us. There is something purely Pompeiian in the contours of the magnificent figures, silhouetted simply in exquisite poise against the darkened background. In it are delicately united the murally decorative spirit of Pompeii and the more perfected realism of the sixteenth century. The lovely figure of Atalanta, clad as the Artemis of the Greeks, turns back in the whirl of the race to gather up the golden apple, just fallen from the hand of Milanion. The swift movement in the man's figure has no modern hurry in it—only sublime calm. It is the gait of a God, not that of a mortal. Half-close the eyes, and imagine that those figures are flying past you : in another moment they will have swept out of the picture ! The composition is a *tour de force* of rhythmical movement, and a model of restraint in artistic expression. Apart from this, the faces are so beautiful ! I wonder if more modern art has ever given us a purer Grecian profile than in the face of this Atalanta ?

The Danae of Titian is perhaps the only bit of colour here sufficiently gorgeous to rival the tints of Nature without, and there is a beautiful Velasquez, a picture that might well symbolise the laughing life of Naples. In it a semi-nude Bacchus crowned with vine-leaves is surrounded by jesting peasants. Redolent of keen animal life are their broadly smiling faces : a marvellous picture, this.

Grouped in front of all the pictures of interest are seated copyists in the midst of their paraphernalia of easels, high stools, and ladders. Sometimes there are so many that it is very difficult to approach the pictures at all. On the arrival of any visitor they endeavour to attract attention to their copies, any of which they are only too thankful to sell for the smallest sum. The faces of some of these artists, who seem to spend their whole day in the cold galleries, are thin and pathetic. All unconsciously they give us a glimpse into the painful poverty of artist life in Naples. They are wonderfully courteous to strangers, and will often help in searching for pictures.

During last year the entire Museum was laboriously cleared out and renovated, and certainly it needed it badly. The management of the place has of late years given rise to many an angry discussion as to the carelessness of the directors and the economising of funds needed for its proper maintenance. Some years ago the Museum of Berlin acquired an object of great value which should certainly have found its way into the Naples Museum. An Etruscan inscription, found in the Campagna, was first offered for purchase here ; but it was judged false, because two specimens offered by the same vendor were found to be spurious, and the third was not even examined.

Adjoining the Museum is a splendid National Library, large, airy, and carefully catalogued. In it is the largest

# Naples—The Museum—Capo di Monte

*Salle* in Italy, containing all the original volumes of the Bourbon collection, and having its stupendous ceiling frescoed with the portraits of the Royal family. Some time ago this ceiling threatened to fall, and for upwards of ten years the hall had to be closed, until the other day the Government finally decided to dole out the necessary funds for its restoration, since the ceiling itself refused to collapse, and so settle the question.

Naples is rich in collections of great value. Not far from the Museum stands the splendid Palazzo Filangieri, containing an exquisitely arranged collection of historic objects, chiefly of the Bourbon period. The Museum itself is, I believe, the oldest thirteenth-century building in Naples, and when it was about to be pulled down to make way for the new street and tram-line Prince Filangieri, at his own expense, removed it brick by brick from one side of the road to the other. It is kept very differently from the Museo Nazionale, and is like a carefully inhabited palace, contrasting with the neglected squalor of many an interior laden with valuables in Naples. The old guardian, who sits in his tiny cubicle, and in the winter months roasts small scented apples over his *scaldino*, often unconsciously perfumes the lofty rooms with their sweet aroma.

Outside the Museum we find our eager *vetturino* on the look-out for us, and screaming and cracking of whips bring us rudely down from dreams of other days. I wonder whether the Pompeiian drivers used such expressive language to their horses as do the Neapolitan drivers of to-day! Or were the noble chariot steeds of the ancients, high-mettled descendants of the breeds introduced by Pyrrhus and Hannibal, treated with more respect and less ignorance?

" In the kingdom of Naples I have observed more horses of high blood than in any other quarter of Italy," remarks the Boccaccio of Landor's imagination ; and the hero of one of Boccaccio's *novelli* is described as coming to Naples to make purchases, having heard that there was a good market for horses in the city. And it is much the same in the present day. Magnificent carriage-horses are seen on the sea drive, while even many of the smaller rapid cab-horses have a fiery step worthy of a better breed.

It is difficult to understand the humour of the Neapolitan cabmen. A lady who was being persistently followed by a pertinacious cab-driver said to him, " But why should I take a carriage? I had a very bad horse yesterday : so to-day I prefer to walk." He answered, with a twinkle of the eye, as of a man who launches his best *bon mot* : " Signora, is your thumb as long as your index ? Is it as long as your other fingers ? Then, why should this horse resemble the one you took yesterday ? " Laughter from the loiterers greeted this remark, showing that it appealed to their idea of the ridiculous, which so often seems unreasonably keener than ours.

If we follow the road up the hill, past the Naples Museum, it will lead to the palace of Capo di Monte. On this beautiful site Charles III. founded his famous porcelain fabrique, and in the palace may still be seen

THE PARK OF THE PALACE OF CAPODI-
MONTE, ABOVE NAPLES

Autumn.

a room lined entirely with flowered pottery, as pretty
as it would be uninhabitable. Charles III. had married,
in 1738, the daughter of the king of Poland, and she
brought with her a quantity of china from the famous
fabrique of Meissen. This seemed to give an impulse
to industry in and around Naples. At that time the
fabrication of porcelain was a secret possessed only
by a young alchemist named Frederick Böttger, who
worked under the protection of the Elector of Saxony.
He had re-discovered it from deep study of Chinese
pottery, and jealously guarded it for the king. It
became the fashion among kings and princes to become
patrons of porcelain factories, and Charles also determined to indulge the taste. Fixing upon the site of
Capo di Monte for his works, after only two months the
building was completed, for the king never permitted
his building projects to be dawdled over. He even
built the church of S. Gennaro, opposite, for the use of
the workers.

When he found himself obliged, in 1759, to go
to Spain, Charles broke up the fabrique he had so
delighted in, took with him all the materials, and
before embarking ordered all the furnaces and offices
to be destroyed, so that not a trace of his secret should
remain. But this jealous egotism brought him little
success. He never succeeded in Madrid with his
pottery, which would not resist the heat : the cups
cracked when filled with hot liquids. A large collection of the porcelain may be seen in the palace, very
flowery and often in bad taste, but yet with a strong

character of its own. His later mark, **R F**, stood for *Real fabrique*,—not for Rex Ferdinandus, as French writers assure us. In 1805 the works entirely ceased, and the French and new Governments conceded the fabrique to private industry. In 1834 it seemed to acquire a new lease of life ; but the awful cholera of two years later threw all industries aside, and so ended the history of the porcelain of Naples.

The palace of Capo di Monte is built over catacombs and said to be somewhat damp, but the park is beautiful. Go there on an autumn day, when the avenues fade away in the distance, when the trees are turning to russet red, and the crisp falling leaves flutter gently in the breeze. In the silence is heard the whistle of the gamekeepers, calling the pheasants to be fed, and now and then a grey-garbed figure with slouching hat and shouldered gun saunters down the vast paths. This enormous park is said to have been inspired by English style ; but, since the English and French pleasure-grounds themselves originated in Italy, Capo di Monte is, as it were, but a revival of the Italian style, on an enormous scale.

# CHAPTER III

WITHIN the last quarter of a century the face of Naples has completely changed. It has changed, not slowly and subtly, as in other old towns, but as if a feverish desire to obliterate the past, as well as to re-model the present, possessed its inhabitants. A city of magnificent hideousness has sprung up, and Naples, once coloured with all the varied styles of the Renaissance, and full of the fine patrician palaces of the fifteenth and sixteenth centuries, has now grown into a colourless map of shadeless streets and un-broken house fronts. The sanitation of the city, not its beautifying, has been the sole object; and the modernising of Naples has been carried out without respecting the natural beauty and character that the life of many centuries had stamped it with. That this is felt by the cultivated Neapolitan himself the monthly publi-cation of *Napoli Nobilissimo* bears expressive witness.[1]

But the appearance of wealth and well-being about the new quarters as compared with the period previous

[1] This paper was started some twelve years ago by Salvatore di Giacomo, and is one of the best periodicals of its kind in Italy.

6

to the 'Sventrimento is really wonderful. The shops are
handsome, and the streets wide. The hired horses and
carriages are infinitely better than of old. The beggars
earn, I am told, upwards of five francs daily during the
season. Perhaps because they no longer beg on horse-
back, as Stendhal boldly asserts that they did in his day!

Each year those who would see the heart of Naples
as it still is must pierce farther into the old quarters,
where Poverty reigns more supremely than in any other
city in the world. That great menagerie of human
beings and four-footed animals, who overcrowd the
old Vicoli, and about which so much has been written
since Mr. Gladstone penned his scathing letters, is now
steadily retreating from the shore, which from time
immemorial has been its rightful pasturage. With this
movement are vanishing the multi-colours, the historic
squalor, the " picturesque smells " of Old Naples. If
the artist grieves that his field has been hopelessly white-
washed, the tourist ought to, and probably does, feel sheer
gratitude. It is far more on his account than on account
of the inhabitants that Naples has been modernised.

But it is surely a pity that the new life of the city
includes changed names for historic streets. It is as if,
with the unity of the country, all traces of past foreign
governments and incidents were to be erased. The
old largi, vicoli, traversi, are haunted with the names
of the past. Why change them? Here is the traversa
Cellini, reminding us that Benvenuto Cellini was in
Naples in 1532, flying from Rome after one of his
many knife adventures. Here is the via named after

# Past and Present—Santa Lucia, Etc.

Giovanni della Porta, that quaint genius to whom no other monument exists. And so on, all over the complex geography of the city. And the Via Toledo, one of the oldest streets in Italy, has been christened anew as if it dated from yesterday. Yet it was the pride of the city, wide and handsome for over a mile, when the Corso of Rome was as narrow as a back street of to-day ; when the Calsaioli in Florence was a lane ; when the great Boulevards of Paris, and the rue Impériale of Lyon were unconstructed. Its existence, too, is as a milestone in the history of Old Naples, for till then there was no street worthy of the name in the kingdom of the Anjous. When Don Pedro first arrived in Naples, horrified at the miserable condition of the roads in his new *royaume*, he determined to build one worthy of his great name. Levying a new and perhaps somewhat cruel excise tax " di un tornese a rotolo su cose da magnare " in spite of the tumultuous protest of the people, he had his way and the street grew.

> ". . . where such had ne'er been dreamt
> Or even thought of, now the sight
> Of noble palaces and swiftly built
> Bid feet pause with delight,
> And all with one accord the words repeat,
> Toledo's new and splendid street," [1]

---

[1] ". . . onde non fui pensato,
Nè si penso giammai, hora si vede
Erte palazzi e presto edificato,
Che di lieta veder ne fermo il piede,
E si noma da ognun, senza altro viete,
La nove e bella strada di Tolete."

wrote the Sappho of that day, Laura Terracina, in her flowery appreciation of Don Pedro and his many works.

Since then the Toledo has been the heart of the gaiety of Neapolitan life, the kaleidoscope of all its human movement and colour. Madame de Genlis, in the eighteenth century, likened it to the rue St. Honoré, which is certainly one of the noisiest streets in the world. It was improved in the time of Murat, during whose energetic but too brief rule the Piazza Ferdinando, which closes the Toledo, was enlarged. Since then the pretentious Galleria Umberto, modelled on the same plan as the galleries of Milan and of Florence, has still further changed this end of the street. The gallery covers the site of the old Largo del Castello, where once stood the Locanda del Signor Monsoni, at which Goethe stopped in 1787.

The sunny and dusty Piazza Plebiscite, with all the parts about it, is full of interest, though not a single feature of the days prior to Charles III. remains unchanged. A statue marked the centre, where now stands the fountain. The Via Chiaia did not exist. On the right, where to-day stands a magasin de nouveautés, "La piccolo Guagagna," stood the once famous Café Europa, where Altavilla, the author of a hundred comedies, wrote his play of that name. Opposite it, where now is seen Gambrinus, stood the warehouse of one Savarese, patronised by Ferdinand II.; and there, on the Giorno dello Struscio, the king used to come to

THE FOUNTAIN OF PAPPARELLA IN
THE VILLA NAZIONALE OF NAPLES

The enormous granite bowl came originally from
Paestum.

# Past and Present—Santa Lucia, Etc.

take refreshments. On Thursday and Friday in Holy Week the Via Toledo is reserved for foot passengers, who swarm there in vast numbers. The sweeping of the women's silk dresses, which they let drag in the dust, gave rise long ago to the now historic name of "Struscio." In the evening, between five and six, the crowd becomes "smarter." Private carriages fill the narrow street; the pavements are packed with Neapolitan ladies and their escorts; Cafliesh, the popular cake shop, is filled to overflowing. What strikes the foreigner is the freedom with which the men make audible remarks about, or stare at, the women. It is a fashion, rather than any deliberate rudeness. A very pretty Frenchwoman, walking down the Toledo with her husband, was so persistently annoyed by an army officer following and staring at her, that her infuriated husband suddenly took some coppers from his pocket and flung them at the admirer. The unfortunate man was deeply chagrined, having supposed that his behaviour was doing the lady the greatest honour.

Across the Piazza stands the Palazzo Reale, which the first Bourbon king restored, decorating it with frescoes and arabesques from his new toy, Pompeii. In the façade of this palace may be read the whole history of Naples, for from its niches not a single Neapolitan looks down from among the statues of the many sovereigns. Looking up at the windows, it is natural to remember that it has been the haunt of fleeing and returning sovereigns, and to recall the days

when a brilliant French court occupied it, the passion
for French titles giving it the ill-omened name of the
Tuileries. The last two Neapolitan kings shared the
same nickname of "Bomba"—the only instance, I think,
of a *nom de nique* inherited.

There is an older palace at the back of the Piazza ;
but nobody remarks it now. Its towers have sunk,
and it is but an empty shell, full, not indeed of ghosts
(for ghosts are extremely rare all over Italy), but of
horrors—skeletons and ghastly legends. Yet the
Castel Nuovo was one of the great achievements of
the Anjous. In it was the famous chapel built in the
Gothic style they introduced, and which was completed
by Robert the Wise, the only king of Naples to whom
a beneficent title has clung. There, between 1329 and
1332, Giotto is said to have painted his frescoes while
the king delighted in watching him at work, listening
to his talk. Not a trace now remains of the bright
genius which once glorified this chapel, said to have
been the most beautiful of the time. That Giotto
really worked there one may reasonably doubt ; still,
the official list of items for the painting of the
ceiling during that period were paid to "Zotto di
Firenze."

Close on the back of the Royal Palace stands San
Carlo, the result of a Nero-like determination to build
the biggest theatre in the world. It sprang up within
three months, as if under the touch of a magic wand,
a "Coliseum of modern times" (as some one called
it), the opening of which roused theatre-going to a

passion. Under the porticoes is still occasionally seen the figure of one of the public writers who since the days of Goethe have been so familiar a feature in Naples. There he sits, often under a tattered umbrella, with his century-old paraphernalia before him. It is an institution which disappears slowly. Schools are still compulsory only in name ; and though army education has lessened illiteracy, and the lottery encourages a knowledge of figures, the very poor are as ignorant of reading and writing as in the days when Ferdinand declared " mon peuple n'a pas besoin de penser."

In the centre of the Piazza Plebiscite stands the great fountain opened by Humbert in 1885, which may be looked upon as the crowning monument of modern Naples. If the ghosts of past generations were to revisit their native town, they would surely pause before this simple marble basin. It marks the boundary between the night and the dawn of its history—between the days of epidemic and disease, of terrible and enforced squalor, of fetid water supply, and to-day, when the water of Naples can hold its own with the classic springs of Rome. To the Neapolitans of our time it is a reminder of the courage and energy of the king in promoting sanitation when the cholera had laid bare all the hideous secrets of the city. He was a benefactor in the widest sense of the word as well as king, and would gladly have been the former only, as is proved by the many stories of his simple tastes. " Ah," said Humbert one day to Madame Serao, " how gladly would I accept a journalist's life were I not king!" The authoress not unnaturally answered, "Were I not a journalist, your Majesty, I would not refuse to be king!"

With the erection of San Carlo, the building of royal palaces about the kingdom (for which the Tuileries at Versailles had revived the fashion), the opening of the Via Chiaia and the Via Chiatamone, which became the principal haunts for the elegant alberghi of that day (as they still are), the journey to Naples became more than ever the fashion. There was much to attract at that time. Vesuvius was gaining a second celebrity with a series of active and beautiful eruptions, and with the discovery of those cities it had long ago destroyed. The days of bloodshed preceding the advent of the Bourbons was followed by a hopeful lull. The Academy was thronged with foreigners, and a revival of art and learning seemed to throb through the unfortunate city. Of all periods of Neapolitan history this is one of the most fascinating, bringing with it as it did all the wit, the beauty, and the learning of foreign countries. Alfieri came hither in his prime, and with his ardent dreams of a future Italy; Goethe philosophised; Angelica Kauffmann tried to paint unsympathetic royalties with as graceful a touch as the subjects allowed; Madame Piozzi wrote her raptures of "dear, delightful Naples"; a whole world of travellers rejoiced in its beauty.

The Bourbons were a poor lot, but the last chapters of Neapolitan court life belong to them, and court life covers a multitude of sins. In spite of all the bloodshed that closed the century, in spite of the enslaving feudalism, the poverty and ignorance of the plebe, the reckless misadministration of justice, and the instability of the throne, there was a wave of hope and promise running through the intellectual life of Naples, which gave it a glow, a colour, a vigour, of which the Unity seems to have robbed it. The city has remained, even in its united prosperity, a deserted kingdom. Even the visits of the king, whose birth and youth belong to Naples, have become rarer and rarer.

"The unity of Italy has enriched the towns of the north and taken nothing from them," said a Neapolitan whose father had fought in the Bourbon army, while his father-in-law was the last representative of the king in Sicily ; "but, for the right to call ourselves Italian, the Neapolitan has given up his kingdom and all he had."

"Naples est la seule capitale de l'Italie ; toutes les autres villes sont des Lyons enfermés," wrote Stendhal.

It is but a step from the Piazza and the modern life of the city to the old steps of the Pallonetta, which lead straight from the rich quarter down into the poorest. These steps form one of the most striking pictures of the old native form of street building ; but they are doomed to disappear with the fishing population which once crowded about them. The bay that washed the house walls below has long been filled up, and with incredible swiftness the great houses and hotels of the

# Naples

Via Lucia have arisen. Beyond the Pallonetta large tenement houses are now seen, built nominally as sanitary homes for the Lucians, but practically so far above their heads in price that the best-off among them could not pay a third of what is asked.

" Yes ; Santa Lucia will have its new houses ; but the Lucians will not change their manner of life. And, what is worse, driven away from the sea, they will feel yet more bitterly the suffering which is the destiny to which the poor are born."

That a strange pathos hangs about the destruction of S. Lucia few will deny. In the gradual civilisation of cities, progress has been slow, almost unfelt, in piercing into the fetid hearts of overcrowded quarters and leaving them pure and healthy. Time has gradually thrown down the useless and put in its place what the life of the day requires. But in this case resolution and action went hand in hand. The terrible epidemic of cholera, the flight of all foreigners, and the utter poverty which followed, awakened the whole country to the truth that the condition of Naples had become a question of national importance. No time could be lost, and the demolishing of this among other crowded centres of a remote past has been carried out within a few years. But in the case of S. Lucia the pickaxe had to be directed at human as well as stone foundations. With the destruction of their homes, a whole race, distinct and proud, has been undermined, for, as the poet has truly said, the Lucians will not live else-where.

CHURCH OF S. CROCE, NAPLES

In the vast piazza in front of it the rag markets are
held, and a great trade is done in old shoe soles.

# Past and Present—Santa Lucia, Etc.

"Santa Lucia! That romantic name which once made those of the most distant shores, of far-off countries, tremble deliciously and dream and think! Lamartine, Dumas, De Musset, Sainte-Beuve, Dickens, Théophile Gautier, and other rare spirits pronounced with emotion those two words which evoke in their tender memories visions of the smiling sea, the clear sunrise, the purple afterglow, sparkling moonlight, emerald reflections, the scraping of soft guitars, the suggestive tinkling of mandolines. O sweet Naples, O blessed soil! Still over all the world the wandering minstrels sing to them in the taverns, the restaurants, under the windows of the inns, on board ship in distant ports. And hundreds of lips repeat in chorus, with a passion which makes the hair rise,

> " ' Mare si lucido
> Lido si caro
> Scordar fa i triboli
> Al marinaio
> Venite al agile
> Barchetta mia
> Santa Lucia, Santa Lucia.' " [1]

This song, which seems so purely Neapolitan, was written by a Frenchman, De Lauziere. Curiously enough, of the two popular songs of Naples, "Santa Lucia" and "Bella Napoli," one was by a foreigner, while the author of the other is unknown.

Whether the Bourbon tax on the shade of trees had

---

[1] *Santa Lucia*, by Ferdinando Russo.

anything to do with the past century's steady destruction of parks in and about Naples, I know not ; but certainly the city, which was once a series of vast gardens reaching from S. Elmo down to the shore, cannot now boast of a single fine park. Turning from the Via Lucia to the sea, we reach the narrow and stunted Villa—as the public gardens are called, with a lingering tradition of Roman days. It is all that remains of the thick and beautiful wood up to the verge of which the waves washed. Near it a great rock rose from the sea, known as the "Scuoglio di Messer Leonardo," of which the old song says :

> " O, how often towards the fall of evening
> Together with thoughtless comrades did we go,
> Above the rock of Messer Leonardo
> To feast upon the cockles from below." [1]

In the garden stands the beautiful Aquarium, the only quiet spot amid the terrific noise of Naples. It was founded some thirty years ago by Anton Dorhn, who won lasting honour by his splendid work, and the institution is supported by the joint contributions of several governments. It is a distinctly cosmopolitan school. All the exquisite contents of the tanks come from the Bay of Naples itself, and it is said that many

[1] " O, quante vota, la sera, a lu tardo
Le 'vemo a spasso cu tanta zetelle
'Ncopp' a li scuoglio de messè Lunardo
E là faciamo spuonele e patelle."

## A BALIA (NURSE) IN THE VILLA NAZIONALE, NAPLES

The public gardens are the rendezvous of all the children and gorgeously dressed nurses on Sunday afternoons.

years' research would not exhaust the fauna of this one branch of the Mediterranean.

The Villa is a pleasant and amusing spot to loiter in, always cool, even in summer. On certain days the band performs, and on the marble seats sit rows of gorgeously dressed balias, some of whom possess costumes quite Titianesque in splendour. The children's parents never seem very far off ; for the Neapolitans are a domestic people—particularly the men. It is interesting to note the great difference of type between the various classes, a difference which is as noticeable in figure as in face. The bourgeoisie are ill-formed, fat, and heavy, even in youth ; the noblesse have types as slender, as nervous, as in the North.

A small café stands among the trees, and a crowd may sometimes be noticed listening with rapt attention to a Neapolitan story-teller, a genuine relic of the days of Boccaccio, whose tales are quite as romantic and highly flavoured. His language, of course, is pure dialect. At the culminating point of the story, when every listener is hanging upon the next word, he abruptly pauses and passes his plate round. Dirty, unkempt, and often totally unlettered as he is, his gestures are those of the born actor, the natural gift of the country that produced Silvio Fiorillo, the possible creator of the Punchinello,—of the land, too, which has pro-duced, with one Italian exception, the best collec-tion of Fairy Tales in Europe—the now-forgotten *Pentamerone*.

Outside the rails of the Villa lies the fine drive, the

# Naples

Via Carraccioli, with its hideous border of hotels. Its name reminds us of an incident which the Neapolitan has not forgotten, and when the descendants of a great name visited Naples they were received with coolness.

It seems to be the fashion among the youth of Naples to drive absurd little carriages drawn by diminutive ponies or donkeys. Only persons of the poorer classes, or an occasional group of urchins, wretched little scunnizzi, on the watch for cigarette ends, pass on foot. On the fête-days, when the small bourgeoisie indulge in hired victorias, they never recognise their pedestrian friends.

Beyond the noisy rush of carriages lies the turquoise sea, a continual delight to the eye and to the senses. "On ne travaille pas à bord de la mer ; on n'y pense pas même. On rêve." How true it is ! On the left, dimly through the trees rises the shadowy form of Vesuvius, about which, I believe, something of the old mediæval belief in the nether world still lingers in Naples. Else why is it the only feature of their country about which the native poets never or rarely write ? During the last great eruption a frate said to a friend of ours, as he gazed across the bay at the burning mountain,—

"Dicono che non esiste l' Inferno ! Allora di dove vien tutto questo fuoco ? "

Far out to sea, like a dim-coloured plover's egg, lies the Castel del Ovo, fastened to the shore by a narrow breakwater. Virgil was said to have founded Naples upon eggs, as a magical charm for its protection, and this legendary derivation may have had some share in the naming of the castle. Round it, in the summer nights, the eels are speared by the light of torches. The subject has inspired one of the most graceful of di Giacomo's *Poems of a Monastery*—the poem of the young acolyte who has taken upon himself a vain vocation :—

> "Under the Castle del Ovo
> The spearing of eels gleams bright,
> And the dim-skinned fishermen light
> Their torches of fiery glow
> Where the prow of the barque dips low
> To search the depths of the night.
>
> "But the all subtle sea
> Lets not its depths divine,
> Lets no heaven wholly shine
> Through its profundity;
> And this convent seems to me
> Deep as the soundless brine.
>
> "For when I gaze around
> I see men on every side
> Who seem to escape me—to hide,
> To be dumb, or to make no sound !
> And I think, even I, ah me !
> Such depths for my life have found." [1]

Unconsciously this may express the new sentiment of our time, in a city whose two hundred monasteries have dwindled down since Ferdinand suppressed the richest to the lingering few of to-day.

Whilst the monastic life is more limited than it was a century ago, the old religious festivals and ceremonies

[1] From the dialect of *Il Monasterio*, di Giacomo.

have changed not a whit. Still does the blood of
S. Gennaro, S. Stefano, S. Giovanno Battista, S. Panta-
leone, and S. Patricia liquefy yearly as in the sixteenth
century, while that of Carafa, Founder of Holy Works,
and of Don Placido Baccher in the Gésu Vecchio remain
ever liquid. The old orders of the Misericordia are
seen continually in the streets, from the aristocratic
order of S. Ferdinando, which in snowy garments
follows the coffins of the upper class, to the humbler
societies who officiate for the poor. But, talking of
funerals, I doubt whether the large affiches bearing the
name of the deceased, which for a certain sum may be
hung above the doors of the church, were customary
a century ago. Surely the mediæval spirit would
have been shocked at the sight of flaring advert-
isements pasted upon the pillars of many of the
churches?

Naples is a city of historic and pauperising charities.
"Il n'y a qu'à Naples, la charité est dans le sang";
and vast sums are spent in helping those who will not
help themselves. But these charities lie far from the
new quarter we have visited. The oldest of all, but
one, is that of the Annunciation, of which the tourist
probably knows little, save that a certain hole in the
wall through which abandoned children used to be
thrust is now closed. But a visit to the building,
though not exactly cheerful, is interesting. Among the
inmates may be seen the last sufferer of that closed-
up hole, a girl who remembers being thrust through
into the revolving case at the age of seven. The

STREET SCENE, THE MARINA, NAPLES

The fruit and vegetables of the town are sold almost
entirely on hand-carts about the streets.

number of infants in this home is quite appalling. Hundreds and hundreds of half-starved babes line the enormous rooms, with one *nourrice* to every five. No child leaves the precincts of the building before eight years of age. The parents may then claim their offspring, a large percentage of whom have *not* been born out of wedlock; but the greater number are never claimed, and remain in the home to master a handicraft. Sometimes some devout youth, in gratitude for an answered prayer, makes a vow to the Virgin to marry one of the humble daughters dedicated to her care. Then the girl on whom such rare fortune smiles goes out into the world of narrow streets and struggling homes with a dot of a hundred francs, which she usually lavishes upon the first feast she has ever enjoyed.

Among the new five-story houses which are rising all over Naples, the old palaces or churches of the Renaissance seem out of place now; but a few corners are left to show us dimly what an exterior or interior in the time of the Anjous was like. The little chapel of S. Pietro dei Minuti, in the Duomo, is perhaps the interior the most intact, in spite of restorations; while the church of S. Maria di Donna Regina (not far from the Duomo), which, passed over by the guide books, is therefore also ignored by the average tourist, is literally filled with treasures of the past. About the church of S. Lorenzo hangs, we know, the peculiar interest of Fiammetta's image, telling us that even Naples, the dissolute city of Boccaccio's day, was

8

capable of producing one of the five mystic types of
the platonic worship of women. In an age when
morals were utterly lax, the ideals who inspired pure
and lasting love stand out with sharp distinctness.
Boccaccio, like Petrarch, first saw his lady in a church.
Like Laura, she was the older of the two, was married,
and in both cases the details of their lives are unknown.
Did Boccaccio really love, or did he but dream another's
dream? We shall never know; but, whether flesh and
blood or only spirit, the type remains to Naples along
with its one other typical figure of a woman—Queen
Joanna, the Neapolitan Semiramide.

"Grassa nè magra, bella, el vizo tendo."

These two opposite types have one link in common, in
that no authenticated statue or portrait of either has
come down to us.

We are in the Syren's city; and it is interesting to
know that, ages past, before the church was built, the
colossal head now known as the Capo di Napoli,
which tradition claims to have belonged to the Syren
Partenope, was discovered here. It now stands in
the Via Eligio, transformed under the inevitable white-
wash of the Risanimento, and with a new nose. So
often has that nose been broken and mended that an
element of the ridiculous has clung to it, and any large-
headed and ill-featured person gives rise to the expression, "Me pare donna Marianna a capo 'i Napoli."

A few of the finer palaces still keep their primitive
forms—such as the Palazzo dei Carafa, in the Via

# Past and Present—Santa Lucia, Etc.

Biagio, and, not far from it, that of Capua, conte di Altavilla;—and not all were built by foreigners, for there *were* a few Neapolitan architects, though even those are sometimes wrongly termed Florentine. In those days Florentine and Siennese painters and architects were so common in Naples that the native craftsman was overshadowed. There is, perhaps, only one case of a Neapolitan artist of that time in Tuscany—a certain Giovanni di Pietro, one of whose frescoes may be seen in Pisa.

Every one has remarked the extraordinary façade of S. Gésu, which, in spite of its latter-day usage, keeps the stern and princely atmosphere of a palace. It belonged to the Prince of Salerno, who made himself a great favourite by giving splendid dramatic entertainments,—for there was no public theatre in the middle ages. Only in the seventeenth century was a regular theatre instituted; under the Spanish rule half of all profits from dramatic entertainments was given to the hospitals.

Naples is now full of theatres—from the Florentine, where Duse acted as a girl in Goldoni's comedies, to the Mercadante, where Scarpetta acts in his own plays: almost the only actor Naples has produced in the last decade,—but the drama is not of a high order, and even that "fanciful folly" which, Disraeli says, finds its way into their extemporary comedy is singularly lacking.

The streets in the direction of S. Gésu and Basso Porto lead into many a poor vicolo, which the sventrimento has not yet reached, and where the cholera once played havoc—or, stranger still, passed over !

> " This is the Fondaco Verde of Basso Porto ;
>   They say 'tis going to be enlarged at last,
>   After so long !   Well, 'tis a good idea
>   To let fresh air into that breathless past.

> " In this alley, ill-paved, tortuous,
>   Where the very sun's rays are denied,
>   During the cholera, two years ago,
>   Only one died, they say, *only one died !*

> " Impossible !   So, if for an instant,
>   Within its misery lost, you would have sworn.
>   Only one dead ?   Yes, but a hundred born.

> " And this greasy, ever-screaming mass,
>   Augment, increase, until to hundreds grown
>   No alley this ; a rank field, ploughed and sown." [1]

Here it is, in these poor streets, that the links between the Naples of yesterday and that of to-day are found— links that will not be broken, though so many of the old landmarks of the city have gone.   De Falco, Celano, and the old guides who centuries ago conducted foreigners through their beloved city, might no longer find their way about ; the character in Dumas's book who could find his way all over Naples in the shade would be at a loss amid the stretches of dazzling squares and streets.   But the old traits and customs remain.   Still is the number of four-footed animals vaster in proportion to the population than in any other city in the world ; still are man and beast

[1] Translated from the Neapolitan of di Giacomo.

TYPES OF PEASANTRY, NAPLES

decorated with horns of coral and silver; the Neapolitan's right hand is constantly in the position of the charm pointing downwards. The screaming and gesticulations of the plebe are as distracting as ever. The street may be wider; but it is still their home, and there they sit and work, or sleep, or perform their toilet with unblushing publicity, spitting right and left the while. Only at night do they retreat into their dark houses, or to eat their fattening diet of macaroni and chestnut-meal soup. Coffee is said to be drunk in greater quantity in Naples than in any other European city. The street is the kitchen, however, rich in colour and smell, for the Neapolitan only cares to eat what he has seen cooked. Nothing in its way is more striking than the autumn cuisine. The roasting of chestnuts is world-wide; but where else are they offered for sale in bouquets, each chestnut spiked upon a short stick? In the middle of a pavement, driving foot passengers into the road, is placed a great stove with a glow of ruddy light about it. On the red-hot wires the gorgeous pepperoni are dancing, roasting for winter consumption. The street itself is often blocked with hand-carts of Indian figs, pomegranates, and mummified packets of grapes, swathed in a lemon leaf, and then again in dried and crackling vine leaves. The scene is beautiful; the dirt, the impure air, and the wretched poverty of the figures around one are incapable of spoiling it. Here is one of the last of the macaroni shops, where the spaghetti is *not* devoured to earn soldi, but from sheer, absorbing hunger. Near it stands a barber's shop.

# Naples

The barber practises bleeding with leeches as of old, and has written over his shop door the absurd inscription—" Fabbrica di Mignetti che si applicano a domicile,"—literally, "Fabrique of leeches which may be applied to the domicile." We are in a hopeless confusion of past and present. The corricolo has disappeared, the lazzaroni are extinct; but the spirit of driving and of begging are unchanged, and I am inclined to think that they never will change. Kindness to animals seems as much a characteristic of race as of teaching, and begging in a tradeless city becomes a trade like any other.

All around, in the midst of deafening noise and the greatest misery, the gaiety of the Neapolitans is more striking than anything else. They are the gayest people in the world, as they have ever been—the same who inspired these words of Sainte-Beuve's : " Il faut rire avant que le bonheur vient, à peur de mourir sans avoir ri."

But it is the great modern Naples, not the old, that attracts the mass of travellers, and the impression borne in upon one after an effort to become acquainted with its objects of interest is really unique. We are in a city where almost nothing older than the last half century is purely Neapolitan. Everything that arrests the eye in its architecture, or about which legends cling, is foreign. What were they in the past, this people whose dead tell us so little? whose monuments are of usurpers, whose churches show the arms of Spanish families, whose nobility has almost dwindled away,

# Past and Present—Santa Lucia, Etc.

whose only history has been one of enslavement in their own country? It matters little now, perhaps. The future certainly is doubly powerful where there has been no developed past, and there is a certain fascination in watching a people naturally so quick cosmopolising themselves and transforming their country with such rapidity.

# CHAPTER IV

## THE NEAPOLITAN CHARACTER—THE LOTTERY—CAMORRA, ETC.

THE Neapolitans are a fanciful and imaginative people ; and about this imaginative quality, at once the charm and the curse of the South, there is something almost volcanic in its intensity and in its vagaries. It can be traced in every path of life, in every line of work. What is the lottery but an instance of it ? How often has this subject been dwelt upon and considered from the point of view of an incurable passion for gambling, a corroding vice, which a by no means blameless Government has not discouraged ! It might be nearer the truth to regard it as the outcome of a people's fantastic imagination. They are the followers of phantoms, the dreamers of vain dreams. They are slaves of poverty whose exalted hopes of freedom buoy them up with the strength to live. The poorest among the very poor are those who hope the most, since they have the most to gain, and to the last day of their miserable lives this hope never fails them.

From earliest times the lottery was always used as a

A FRUIT SELLER, NAPLES

means of supplying the country's exchequer ; the excuse offered for making use of such a system being that, as the spirit of gambling *always* exists, it should be given a legal outlet. Originating in Spain, the lottery spread and rooted itself over Italy, and was once in the sixteenth century adopted even in England as a source of revenue. But with the progress of civilised ideas its abolition was inevitable ; and that it should still linger in Italy, a system no longer of our time and civilisation, is one of the ills which (to use an expression of Villari's) "eat into the country's spine."

It has been said that were the Government, in whose hands it has been since the Unity, to suppress the lottery, a revolution would ensue ; yet when the French abolished theirs, in 1836, the act was followed by an increase of savings, money banks, etc. No : the Italian Government depends upon and encourages the evil, and if there is the least falling-off in the lottery gains in Naples it exclaims with horror, "What ! are they so poor now that they cannot even play ?"

If there is one method more than another (apart from the interference of the fattened Government) which suggests itself as a possible remedy for the evil, it is that of the influence of the Church. But here arises a new difficulty ; for the lottery is looked upon as being under the special protection of the priests, and there is an erroneous belief that it was founded by Ignatius Loyola himself. Thousands of players habitually stake on the Virgin's numbers, those who win returning thanks as devoutly as the losers curse their favourite Madonna.

# Naples

Dr. Newman maintained the thesis that the profane oaths used habitually by Italians proved that the objects of devotion were ever present in their minds: if this be so, their gambling is inextricably mixed up with their hopes of heaven,—but another instance of their imaginative hopefulness.

Most novel-readers of to-day have read Mathilde Serao's powerful work, *Il Paese di Coccagna*. But books treating of a country's evils are generally more popular with foreigners than with the inhabitants themselves, and the lesson it sought to convey has had no result whatever in Naples itself. As an effort to bring it home more realistically to all classes, Madame Serao consented to the dramatising of her work, without, I believe, profit to herself. The result was a strange one, and throws a high light upon the Neapolitan character. The entire audience enthusiastically wrote down the numbers played by the fictitious gamblers on the stage, and rushed off by hundreds to stake them in that week's lottery. The numbers all came out, and the play had a success such as had never been dreamt of by the authoress.

The strange workings of fate in the Lotto are in harmony with the fantastic history of Naples. In one case its story is interwoven by a mere twist of fortune with those days of cholera which transformed it into a great "Mourning City." In 1884, towards the close of the hot August of that year, a few cases of cholera made their appearance; but they were so carefully isolated that the trouble seemed held in check. On the last

# The Neapolitan Character, Etc.

Saturday of the month a sudden wave of delight swept over hundreds of the poor, who had, as usual, risked their all in that week's lottery. It was not a big gain, —only a few francs each, a "piccolo guadagno," as they call it ;—but it broke the long strain of perpetual disappointment. The drawing of the numbers, as everybody knows, is gone through on the last day of the week, and there is all the idle morrow on which to waste, if not to venture again, the trifle gained. So this vast horde of wretched poor caroused that night and all the next day on a surfeit of unaccustomed food—the over-ripe fruit and vegetables of the hot town. A week later there were five hundred cases of cholera, and no longer a hope of arresting the awful disease.

As the week closes, statistics show a distinct increase in petty theft, especially among the servant classes. They will steal far more readily to play in the Lotto than to spend directly upon themselves. Indeed, the vice of gambling is at the root of a vast quantity of thefts and petty crimes which are roughly classed as camorristic. Think of the temptation ! Impossible to go out without passing a Banco Lotto, with its five flaming red, blue, and green numbers, ticketed up outside,—for each bureau makes its own guess at lucky numbers for the next draw. Habitués, however, often play persistently for years upon the same numbers.

The fortunes of chance are certainly a more curious study in the Italian lottery than even in the frantic play of Monte Carlo. The statistics point to a kind of

permanent luck in certain towns over others, quite
apart from the population and the sums ventured—
chances far beyond even a system. They point out,
too, the phenomenon that it is the seaport towns that
are most prone to play, and on the whole with the
least success. Fortune smiles on Rome and Palermo ;
but towards Naples, whose vast masses of poor venture
their centimes with such unchanging hopefulness, she is
far more capricious.

The strange coincidences of fate meet us right and
left. A money-lender in the Rete File was robbed in
broad daylight. His safe happened to be unlocked for
the moment, and all its contents were taken and he
himself so severely wounded by the gang that he was
left for dead. When he came to, and realised that
he was ruined, in despair the wretched man turned to
his dictionary of lottery numbers, and put the few
francs remaining to him on the three numbers corresponding to an attempt at murder, theft, and unlocked
safe. He won, and recovered every penny lost by his
misadventure.

It seems natural enough, in speaking of the lottery,
to touch also on the other great evil of Naples, the
Camorra. Like the lottery, it is an evil imported from
Spain, that country to which Naples seems to owe
everything rooted in it, good, bad, indifferent. The
Camorra is said to be a direct imitation of a secret
society there, the Guardaba, founded in 1417 at Toledo
by Spanish brigands and galley slaves, which spread so
easily over the South that one cannot but think that the

# The Neapolitan Character, Etc.

Neapolitans were only too well prepared to imbibe its principles. The full meaning of the word "Camorra" (or "Honoured Society," as the Camorristi call it) is probably known only by the Neapolitans themselves, those who benefit and those who suffer from it. Its object is, roughly speaking, to protect criminals, and to benefit in common from their thefts. It is, of course, a paradox to speak of this society as secret. The police know all its members, and, alas! find it only too wise to preserve friendly relations with them. Its ranks are recruited from among mere youths of the lower class, who too easily fall under its evil influence, and can never afterwards free themselves. Nearly all the cab-drivers of Naples are under the control of the "Capo Camorristi" (as the head of the Camorra is styled), and they are easily identified by the square cut of their hair over the ears.

This society may change its name in time, and lose something of its power; but I question whether it will ever be entirely swept out of Naples. It is in the blood of this apparently ground-down people to assert themselves and govern in some form or other. It seems to be the opinion among foreigners of to-day who have lived long in Naples that no Camorra as a society now exists. They say that the word has become a mere term to express all acts of dishonesty, private or political. The Neapolitans themselves, the bourgeoisie, tell another story, and I recall the words of the great historian of Naples: "Italy may indeed continue as entirely free, may have her Budgets as perfectly balanced as she choose, and yet may remain a nation destitute of moral significance. She requires, then, a new ideal, and that ideal cannot be other than social justice, which she should apply before it is demanded. The man who lives in the midst of slavery, side by side with the poor and disinherited, without reacting against the causes of that slavery and that misery, is a man unworthy of his own freedom, and must sink inevitably into moral degradation. In such a case, the Camorra, the Mafia, the brigandage will always exist, and will eat into the marrow of the country's spine." [1]

It would be somewhat bold for any foreigner to assert that he knows, or completely understands, the Neapolitan people. To know any people well there must be, perhaps, some foundation of sympathy or tastes in common ; but the foreigner's sympathy for the Neapolitan people may be said to be very small. Their absolute incapacity to express fact or opinion tersely is alone a barrier. An Englishwoman, herself married to a Neapolitan, holds the amusing theory that the language of the South is so constructed that it is almost impossible to form a sentence without a dubious meaning. Every word slips into the next ; every word is but half pronounced.

Is it a language that will ever die out, and with its disappearance would the Neapolitan himself undergo a change? I can hardly imagine the one without the other, and confess to a secret liking for that illusive dialect that can express at once so little and so much—

[1] Villari.

A CORNER IN THE GARDEN OF LORD
ROSEBERY'S VILLA, POSILLIPO

# The Neapolitan Character, Etc.

a language which, if the voice be soft, is so musical and
passionate, as one may perhaps venture to say that all
Italian dialects are. It has, too, its own literature, its
many dictionaries, even its grammars. It is the chosen
language for the modern poetry and for the drama of
Naples ; but, alas, few others than the natives themselves can understand it, and it is as Sanscrit to the
Roman and the Tuscan. Compare the styles of those
Neapolitan writers who use both dialect and Italian, and
one is more than ever impressed with the natural fitness
of the former for expressing their peculiar types of mind.

Of the dialect poetry much could be written.
Comparing it with the work of Pascarelli, whose
exquisite sonnets in Roman dialect are well known,
Mathilde Serao claims that both the Neapolitan poets
of to-day, Russo and di Giacomo, touch depths of
passion that the Roman writer knows not. But I should
be rather inclined to say that their passionate feelings
were of a different order, verging on a quickly exhausted
violence, and therefore easier to express than the far
more reserved feelings of the North.

A distinct vein of melancholy may be traced in the
Neapolitan literature of to-day. Some trace it back
to the Revolution ; but in the prose works of di
Giacomo at least the influence of the French school
can be detected. It is in his poetry that he touches
a purely original vein, showing a profound knowledge
of the complex human nature around him. This
poet, still a young man, writes his prose in Italian
and his poetry in dialect. The one, therefore, has been

translated, and has spread into France ; but the other, in which his true talent lies, is, so far, too little known.

As far as the Neapolitan drama goes, most clearly can the French influence be traced there, but in a diluted and impoverished form. The theatres of Naples seem to me at a very low ebb. The playwright-actor, Scarpetta, is not strong enough to revive it to full life ; but he has instilled into it his quaint humour, bold and confident acting, and immensely improved scenic display. His plays treat of the bourgeoisie, who are easier to parody than the noblesse, but somewhat tiresome in the very truthful nature in which he depicts them. The one really original work to which Scarpetta can lay claim as an author is the piece entitled *La Miseria e Nobilta*. There is in it a macaroni scene which would alone endear it to the Neapolitan mind. But one is struck in all dialect plays here by the quantity of talking, compared with the dramatic movement. The voices of the Neapolitan actors, when not actually screaming, are so strangely monotonous, their enunciation so rapid and restless, that attention is apt to flag. The history of Scarpetta himself is striking enough. By sheer energy he has risen from poverty to wealth. He is the owner of several palaces. and villas, from which extravagance has from time to time driven him. Up on the Vomero may be seen the villa on which Scarpetta had written the gay inscription, " Qui rido io." But a temporary change of fortune changed it suddenly into " Qui ridiamo noi," when the bailiffs occupied it.

# The Neapolitan Character, Etc.

Scarpetta's popularity in Naples is immense, and there popularity means success, for in Naples everything is "popular" in the way of art and literature. Poet and writer, artist and sculptor, poor as they too often are, must seek to be appreciated by the mass, since there seems to be no distinctly critical and intellectual centre in Naples, as there is in Paris or Rome,—no stern but beneficial ideal for the arts as understood by the few. Has Naples ever produced an art critic? I hardly think so. The few exceptions who stand apart from the popular celebrities of the city are those who carry their work abroad and find there a correct level for it in the criticism of other countries. One of the sculptors best known abroad is Iarace, who has really great power and a fertile imagination. In his studio on the Corso may now be seen a cast of a famous statue representing the conversion of St. Augustine by his mother, a work full of profound subtlety of treatment and an exquisitely refined invention. As an example of the ruinous effects of Neapolitan popularity I might instance a well-known and brilliant sculptor who struck a popular note some years ago, which the foreign critic might well pronounce to have been his death-blow as far as further production went. An exquisite little bust of a girl's head so struck the people's fancy that the artist seems now to spend his time in turning out endless copies of it! It pays. That is the great thing.

There is another quality which is dangerous to the

just appreciation of gifts. That is the Neapolitan's praise of everything of his own country. He rarely compares it with foreign work ; feeling, perhaps, that the more roughly handled are his countrymen and their capacities, the more he must stand up for them. And this habit is more unfortunate than may be at first imagined. Not only does it affect his appreciation of the arts : it also blinds his judgment in politics and detracts from the value of his opinions. He will stand up for the justly attacked as frankly as for the wrongly abused, feeling (with some justice, but no excuse) that in his united country he has by far the hardest struggle to keep in the political running morally and intellectually.

The *Mattino* is a most remarkable case of journalistic enterprise which is popular through its own merits. Its editor, Scarfoglio, had the inspiration of founding in Naples a journal of which the literary scope and standard were to be on an altogether higher plane of excellence than anything of the kind in the country. Taking it out of the atmosphere of petty local gossip, he boldly wrote over the heads of the people who composed his reading public. His collaborators objected on the ground that it was useless to write articles of a sort that were not demanded by the mass who were likely to sub-scribe to the paper. But Scarfoglio was firm in his determination to uphold his standards. "They will come to us in time," he said. "We shall not go down to them." Success favoured his enterprise. His power of political polemics was so great, and the management

## A TERRACE IN THE VILLA ROSEBERY

This villa was formerly known as the Villa de la
Hante.

of the journal so efficient, that he soon made his paper a powerful organ, raising it to a position unique in South Italy. Scarfoglio is a man singularly gifted with the power of political invective, a terrible adversary, whose philippics fall unsparingly on whosoever may cross his path. During the period when his gifted wife collaborated with him, the *Mattino* was in the hands of perhaps the two ablest writers in their separate lines in all Italy. As indicating the manner in which he tempts the public taste away from the usual *feuilleton*, I may mention that during our stay in Naples last summer, he was giving a translation of " Tristram and Iseult." He is a great authority on Provençal literature.

The material difference between the upper and the lower classes is wider in this country than in any other, and the same may be said of their tastes. Music is loved far more by the plebe than by the noblesse. It used to be a common saying that the upper classes went to see and not to hear the opera, and that this is still the case a single visit to San Carlo in the height of the season will suffice to prove. The talking is incessant, and the fashion of paying visits from box to box shows in what spirit the music is regarded. It is still the excuse for a réunion, precisely as it was in the days of Charles III. The Italians keep the passion for first nights which so struck Stendhal, and the least wealthy will gladly pay exaggerated prices for a seat. These first nights are the occasion of jealous competition among the ladies of the audience as to who should receive the most visits from their friends.

# Naples

Even as an accomplishment music is little taught now,
and as a serious study is quite neglected. But the South
is the very home of light song and melody ; and as long
as only the heart is touched and the ear charmed, as long
as no profound feelings are roused, and a too intellectual
attention called upon, all classes delight in music with
an *abandon* quite unknown elsewhere. It is very much
the same with their native poetry, which is full of
"religion, de la tendresse, et de l'amour," but often
lacks depths of thought and sustained feeling. Perhaps
it is from the absence of these qualities that the enchanting
talent for improvising arose, " qui séduit parfois la pensée,
mais ne la satisfait point," and leaves not a trace behind.
But during the last fifty years this transitory form of art
has diminished, the last improviser of real merit being,
I believe, the beautiful Marchesa Palomba.

And the Naples salons of to-day? Read the
descriptions by Stendhal. They are as true as if the
ink on the charming and chosen words were still wet.
The social gatherings are as grandiose as when the
Neapolitan noblesse adorned their own court. The
*apparence* of court life is still in their very blood.
Redolent of the past in so many ways, the illusion is
enhanced by that characteristic of old times—dirty
and ill-kept streets, reaching the very doors within
which lofty and carpeted stairs lead to the great salons.
The entertainments are strictly formal. Few are the
afternoon calls ; there is none of the delightful informal
society of other towns—no dropping in to tea, no
finding friends unawares. And it is curious to see

76

# The Neapolitan Character, Etc.

in this great city so small a remnant of the ancient families who all know one another, and have so often intermarried, yet, for the most part, meet ceremoniously. This comes not from a lack of hospitality, but from old tradition which is so deeply rooted here. To keep open house has never been the custom in Italy, and whatever is true of Italian society in general is equally true of Naples, with the difference that many of its social customs have perhaps been less changed by foreign influences. For though foreigners pour through this city, and hospitality, real and gracious, is offered them—though they are received with "une politesse parfaite, comme cinq cents étrangers ont été avant moi, comme deux cents seront reçus l'année prochaine"—the foreign element leaves, one might almost say, no trace behind. The Neapolitan world changes slowly. It intermarries but little with other countries. It is enveloped still—so it impressed us—with the courtly but now fictitious legends of the past. Many of the noblesse are poor ; but they have a deeply-rooted pride, and the worship of money without birth, which characterises other parts of Italy, is more restrained in Naples.

"The *nouveaux riches* have money, it is true," said a Neapolitan to me ; "but can they have *finesse* ? Ah, no : that is ours ! "

I longed to discuss the value of freshly-made money from the purely practical point of view, balancing its tremendous power, its modernising influences, its frank vulgarity, against this pride of birth that will not permit a fresh start in life without losing prestige ; but I feared to insist. And this reminds us that round many of the old and splendid palaces of Naples a peculiar gloom seems to hang to-day. Only a few of them have remained in the hands of the rightful family owners. It has often struck me that these great ancestral dwellings have had a profound influence on the social life of Italy. Here are a people born (as it were) with a palace on their backs, from which they cannot be torn without an apparently vital injury. For, as I have said, money-making is contrary to the accepted creed of the Neapolitan noble. He cherishes no reviving hope of being able in time to redeem his home, no ambitious determination to set his shoulder to the wheel and wrest his halls from the detested bourgeoisie into whose hands everything sacred seems to fall. Poverty is hard enough to struggle against ; but tradition and poverty together are well - nigh insurmountable.

The Neapolitan families of to-day, whose palace homes have fallen into the hands of the parvenus, find dwellings elsewhere ; but do they ever find homes ? Their social life is still so entirely a growth of tradition that for the moment the impoverished noblesse seem paralysed. This is keenly noticeable in Naples, and the fact that the rich bourgeoisie are parsimonious and entertain but little (while even if they did keep open house the noblesse would never dream of entering) makes the society of to-day somewhat complex.

It is now so peculiarly admissible to discuss from

# The Neapolitan Character, Etc.

mere impressions the characteristics of unfamiliar countries that I may add that to the foreigner the nature of the Neapolitan youth is curiously striking. He seems to lack all vigour, all enthusiasm—to mature before he has dreamed the glorious and ambitious dreams that youth has the right to revel in. If he is poor—the best opening, after all, for talent—he is ashamed to work. If he is the heir to estates, they hamper him, or he them, for he brings to their management an indolent and often obsolete knowledge.

Neapolitans require wonderfully little to amuse them in society, and stand far less in that constant need of fresh entertainment which is the burden of all Saxon hostesses. Their own light and insouciant conversation is sufficient to amuse them, and an evening reception will pass easily without a single song. Sometimes beautiful faces are seen among the women, the fine dark eyes being their chief beauty. Many wear the latest Parisian clothes, and among the upper classes are seen slim and exquisite figures. They have a charming manner—not exactly naïve, but full of natural ease. Their tastes and many of their opinions strike us at first as being wonderfully modern; but beneath the surface they are not yet in harmony with the changed tenor of thought. Society is still narrowed intellectually as of old by the standpoint from which the men regard the women, a standpoint so low that for a woman to be originally gifted and liberal in her ideas is a fact incapable of arousing the least appreciation among her entourage. Among this class of women

—a growing one now—there may be traced a restless
discontent with the stagnation of ideas around them ;
but this is still accompanied by a passionate attachment
to their country, and a nostalgia when away from it,
which binds them closely to the spot.

All Neapolitan women, frivolous or serious, are
devoted to their children, and delight frankly in their
large families.   Men who look little over twenty have
often several children, and a large share of the conversation in the salons is devoted to this subject, which is not
exactly intellectual, while the presence of children at meals
is often a serious restraint.   Among the younger women
fresh ideas are appearing.   A more finished education
is theirs ; they speak several languages ; and though, as
I once heard a well-known artist remark, "women learn
languages, but have nothing to say in them," it makes
them less dependent than of old, and infinitely more
pleasing, given that their sphere is still only to please.
They have also developed a love of out-door life—a real
emancipation in itself.   But in Naples everything novel,
however harmless, has to fight against narrow prejudice, and a pleasure expressed in an out-door walk
is as easily as not misinterpreted into a questionable
"rendezvous."

Once away from Naples, as we rolled northward and
traversed the plains and the snow-covered mountains,
the souvenir of this light and listless city, of the bon-
hommie and the hospitality of the friends we had
left behind, touched more than one responsive chord.
Contrasted with the sterner North, it was like a mirage

VENUS' BATH

A corner of the fantastic and rococo park of Caserta.

of a lighter world than ours ; and it seemed hard to realise, as we looked from our carriage window at the bleak moraines of the St. Gothard, that so short a time before we were lunching on some sunny garden terrace with orange-trees and palms about us and a gentle autumn breeze fanning our cheeks. The ringing laugh of the contadini is still in our ears, and the languor of the South follows us from afar !

# CHAPTER V

"How changed is Nature from the Time antique !
The world we see to-day is dumb and cold ;
It has no word for us.   Not thus of old
It won heart worship from the enamoured Greek."
                                        E. C. LEFROY.

NAPLES lies like a shield between the land of Homer
and of Virgil, of dim traditions and earth-bound
mysteries, and the land of whose history Vesuvius has
silently kept the record.   One side is thickly peopled,
and villages have sprung up one above the other.
Westward, on the contrary, gardens have taken the
place of dwellings, vineyards have spread over ruins,
and a semi-solitude in many a spot has changed the
old character of the coast-line.   It has slipped back
(as it were) from the once luxurious life of the Romans
into a tacit sympathy with Homeric legend.   The
lakes, the dead craters, the steaming breath of sulphur,
the hollow passages and re-echoing caverns,—these
still hold their own in the midst of a wild Nature only
partially disturbed by tourists.

82

## THE VILLA GALLOTTI, POSILLIPO

An exquisite park, in which stand summer and winter villas. A tablet on the wall of the former records the date of the sojourn here of the German Emperor.

# To the West of Naples

This road, which, after branching off towards
Fuorigrotta, is so curiously different in character from
the country to the east of Naples, is far more enjoyed by
those who have some previous knowledge of its history.
There is about it a monotony that requires the touch
of story ; and to instil interest in the humble villages
of our day the guide-books have to draw largely on
their Greco-Roman origins, surfeiting the reader on
the names of the great degenerate Roman age which
so delighted in this peculiar scenery.

But the sea road from Naples to Posillipo is as gay
and delightful as can be, bordered by many a crowded
osteria, brightly painted and vine-clad, and by little wine-
shops cut into the soft tufa rock and decorated with the
withered and meaningless bough which is now all that
remains of the old-time ivy branch sacred to Bacchus.
We pass along the only really clean road in Naples, the
fine sea-drive leading from the Villa Nazionale past
Piedigrotta and on beyond Pozzuoli. Though this is
the fashionable promenade for the Neapolitan of every
class, it is infested with beggars, deformed and horrible
to witness, who seem literally to glory in the misery
they thrust under the eyes of every passer-by.

Here at random is one wretched case. We saw a
boy in rags which held together simply because they were
more or less incrusted into the body. His head was
bleeding profusely from a blow, and he was yelling with
mingled pain and the thirst for revenge. A crowd
collected, of course ; and we paused to see what could
be done, when to our relief two sisters of the poor

appeared upon the scene. They also paused, and listened reflectively to the boy's screams.

"He should certainly bind up his head with cold water," said one.

"But, Sister, the water might be full of microbes," protested the other.

"We had better leave him alone," said both; and they went off. In despair we took the child into the nearest pharmacy; but, at the sight of such an object of filth, the chemist, nearly fainting, hurriedly turned him out with a direction to go to the Piedigrotta Hospital. By this time we felt quite ill enough to go there ourselves!

A man with both legs bound up like those of a mummy used to sit at a safe corner for many hours every day. One evening a charitable stranger threw him a few soldi as he passed. Looking back, he saw the man loosen his bandages, roll them up under his arm, and unstiffen his legs, before walking away.

"So you aren't lame at all, my friend?" said the amused stranger. "Do you think it is an honest way of earning your living, sitting there and doing nothing?"

"*Nothing*, indeed!" growled the man in astonishment. "*You*, Signore, would not think it nothing to sit in one position all day long with these dirty bandages round your legs!"

Certainly, the scenes of poverty follow us from one end of Naples to the other, but where, even here, did Taine see those unfortunate poor who could afford only one shoe to walk about in?

OLD PAVILION OF THE LAGO DI
FUSARO

Built by the Bourbons, and now falling into decay.

# To the West of Naples

The church of Piedigrotta, which lies to our right before we reach the Grotto itself, is extremely old in its history. Boccaccio, in a letter written to a friend from Naples, swears by " the Madonna di Piedigrotta," showing that it must have been a common enough term in the fourteenth century. The name itself may have arisen from the lowness of the near Grotto, which admitted at one time foot passengers only.

But it was not until Charles III.'s time that the famous Parade, which may be seen represented in two pictures of the eighteenth century in the Museum of San Martino, was instituted. It lasted on and off till 1860, when, I believe, Garibaldi intervened and its character was changed. The poetic feature of the great Festa belongs, however, to a time only about half a century ago. Until 1835, at least, nothing approaching a chorus had existed ; and the sudden birth of it in that year is sufficiently illustrative of the wild enthusiasm of the Neapolitan people, and the way in which a small incident will arouse it.

There lived at that time a certain Don Rafaello Sacco, born in 1787, who had grown up in the very midst of the horrors of the closing century. He loved to improvise light verse ; but the writing of poetry was no more a lucrative business in those days than it is now in Naples, where the two best-known and most popular poets cannot draw a livelihood from their works. So Sacco took to the study of optics, and became celebrated for the invention of a machine directed towards discovering forgeries in stamps, seals, signatures, and so on, though from time to time he still improvised and cherished his poetic ambitions. One evening (it was in August 1835) he announced to his friends that he had written a new song, which Donizetti had put to music. There happened to be at that time a tenor enjoying a great *furore* in the Teatro Nuovo, who was paying court to a lady. To the house of this lady Sacco repaired one evening with the tenor and other comrades, to indulge in a little music. The great singer sang love-song after love-song with his eyes sentimentally fixed upon his hostess, and when he had exhausted his repertoire it was suggested that Sacco's little song should be tried. It was called "Te voglio bene assaie," and as the last notes died away the audience rose, beside themselves with delight. Over and over again the song was sung. All present joined excitedly in the chorus, and those who passed in the street stopped and took part. In the early hours of the morning it was still being sung by men, women, and children as though a resistless frenzy had seized the populace, and over and over again the words of the chorus echoed through the streets :

> " Quanno so fatto cennere,
> Fanno me chiagnarraie,
> Te voglio bene assaie
> E tu non pienza a me." [1]

---

[1] " When ashes and dust I shall be,
Let fall on my tomb a tear,
You who to me are so dear
Yet give not a thought to me."

## TORRE DEL GRECO

This white and glittering town has an almost oriental character.

# To the West of Naples

Thus was born the first song of Piedigrotta, and no other has ever had so great a success, though in 1863 Perullo, a young and shortlived poet, had almost an equal triumph with a song which reached even Paris. Tosti, Costa, Denza, and many others have composed Piedigrotta music; but the poetic character of the Festa has now become a mere farce.[1]

Following the sea-line, we soon leave on our right the grotto of Posillipo marked at either end by a poet's tomb. Far above it is the little "Columbaia," too often described to need repetition. "Si vous avez jamais vu un bout de muraille ruinée, c'est la même chose." But it is the magic of the name which naturally holds those who visit the spot for the first time,—the name of the great Augustine poet who first lightened the gloom of the Homeric legend, introduced into the parts we are visiting the doves of Venus and the vision of the Golden Bough, and filled the Elysian fields with the immortal spirits of the good made happy. About no grave, surely, has such frantic worship hovered. He was the sage, the wizard before whose tomb Christian and Pagan alike prostrated themselves. From his *Æneid* the future was consulted. At one time, indeed, this work was held far less as the work of a poet than as that of a magician, and when opened at random, where the finger touched the page—there was the oracular response. From the very day he died legends collected round the name of Virgil. No doubt this originally sprang from the subjects of which his works treated, the knowledge he gave of the Sibyl's

[1] See article by di Giacomo in *L' Illustrazione Italiana*, October 1899.

Cave and of the Sibylline books; while the exaggerated legends which accumulated about his memory in the Dark Ages point to the especial estimate which the people of those times formed of all science and learning. Strabo, Plato, all the writers of the great past developed with them into beings endowed with superhuman gifts.

At the farther end of the Grotto is the tomb of Leopardi, a great poet to whom Italy has never done full justice, perhaps because he lived in that magic age, between 1815 and 1850, which produced so great a wealth of poetry of various countries that its poets almost overshadowed one another. Dusty and dark as is the passage which divides these two tombs, it is a great improvement on the old grotto of Virgil's magic which was so pitch-black that only by shouting "Alla montagna" or "Alla marina" did the waggons avoid bumping into one another. There is still much of the mysterious in these old grottoes and caverns of past ages when the passing through a hole or rock signified the new birth.

The grand ruin of Donna Anna Caraffa is a striking sight on the road to Posillipo. It seems literally to hang over the water. Parts of it indeed threatened to topple into the sea some years ago, and the poor fisher-folk who inhabited crannies of it were advised to leave. It has been patched up and restored to the happy fate which sooner or later overtakes the historic buildings of the past, and is now a pleasant hotel. Beyond it lies villa after villa, a perfect wealth of beautiful private properties, making this one of the most delightful drives

## CAMALDOLI, ABOVE NAPLES

An old seat within the precincts of the convent.
Autumn sunset.

about Naples.  The Gallotti property is perhaps one
of the most typical of the real Italian garden which
is still free from foreign influence.  About it lingers
the peculiar sentiment which the Italian of past days
breathed into his environs—something at once austere
and romantic which has disappeared with his increasingly
cosmopolitan tastes.  What is romance ?  In the present
day, when we have it no longer yet feel it so intensely,
the very word seems to express all that our age has lost.
It is a revelation to turn sharply from a noisy and dusty
world, from a hot and sun-beaten road, into so enchanted a pleasure-ground as this.  Every step leading
down the hill past the winter villa into the cool shade
of the sea-bound terrace and verandahs of summer
opens vista after vista of silent beauty.  It seems like a
fairy world ; and when, from behind bars let into the
moss-grown rock-side, we saw a yellow panther glaring
at us with serpentinely twisted head, it seemed more
natural than strange—as natural as though Circe, tall
and straight, had bid us quaff a cool draught from her
cup on that warm autumn day.

Beyond this garden a road on the right leads down
to the Villa de la Hante, now the property of Lord
Rosebery.  This lies within a garden of quite another
character and with a totally different kind of beauty.
It is as full of flowers as of trees.  There are even
carpets of spring flowers under their shade, and the
smooth paths themselves are as velvet under the feet.
The grounds seem to have grown (as it were) towards
every point of view of the lovely bay, as a sunflower

grows towards the sun. There are endless vistas on straggling heights where a stone seat or bench invites the dreamer. It is, in fact, a very spot to dream in ; the very antithesis in its spirit to unrest.

The road now winds somewhat inland, and comes out opposite to the little island of Nisida, five miles from Pozzuoli, and composed, like the hills of Posillipo, of tufa. It is, according to a brilliant writer of to-day, the peacock's eye in this land of craters or round eyes. It is the long-shaped island not very near or very far from the abode of the Cyclops, covered with woods and wild goats and barren of men and human traces, where Odysseus found a pleasant harbour. In Roman days it was the isle of mystery and retreat, where a few rich families had their summer villas and enjoyed the chase.

The beautiful hazy isle follows us now all round the bay of Baiæ past Bagnoli, which was, I believe, the birth-place of one of the many reputed inventors of the ther-mometer, Sebastian Bartolo. The shore about here was considered for a long period so malarious that when the dwellings of the Chiaja fisher-folk were judged too great an eyesore for the Corso, and a large building was erected for them here, such a fiat of certain death aroused popular indignation and the building was never completed.

In Bagnoli lived, too, a certain Monseigneur Sanfelice, who revived the taste for constructing the manger at Christmas time. It was a fashion which started in the time of Charles III. and only died out half a century ago. All the noble families of his reign delighted in it, while

VIEW TAKEN FROM THE GROUNDS OF
THE VILLA ANTONIETTA, QUISISANA

Now known as the Hotel du Parc.

the Queen herself used to make the shepherds' garments in the palace of Caserta. The fashion even influenced art, and not a few among the sculptors and painters of the time are better known by their mangers and cattle than by their other works.[1]

Pozzuoli—a town which seems thrust by the Solfatara on to the very edge of the sea, and faces across the bay the site where Baiæ stood, "the pride and the shame of Ancient Rome"—occupies a large slice of space in the guide-books. The modern traveller in Italy is, as Ruskin points out, often called upon to admire what he cannot enjoy, and of no spot are the words truer than they are of this. A few miles farther on we turn to the right by the lake of Lucrinus and drive to the grassy sward near the lake of Avernus.

This spot has quite lost its classic disrepute, and a stone border circling it holds in check the waters which once rendered the fields about so malarious. It looks now more like a great artificial pond than the mirror of centuries. On a warm summer day, when the insects are buzzing and butterflies fluttering about its edge, when the sun is shining brilliantly over the lake and catching the soft reflections of the ruined baths on the farther side, there is about it much the same sentiment, half poetic, half artificial, which is often felt in a private

---

[1] In February of this year a very curious Italian crèche of the 18th century was sold at the Hôtel Drouot in Paris. It contained about 175 little Neapolitan dolls, of which the heads, modelled in terra-cotta and painted, were masterpieces of delicate workmanship. Unfortunately, no amateur was found to purchase it, and the dolls were finally sold separately, fetching in all a total of 1525 francs.

park. But the dim grotto of Avernus leading from the edge of the water into the heart of the mountain is still sufficiently pregnant in spirit of the past, though the sensation of following an ink-black and dust-charged passage by the light of smoking torches blends a large share of the purely disagreeable with the mysterious. Sometimes we feel that in visiting these gloomy caverns of other ages we may perhaps catch a faint echo from the secrets of antiquity ; but I question whether we ever succeed. The poetry of the powers of darkness is lost to us of to-day. Darkness was ever the colour that ignorance took in the past, and science and discovery have now thrown such head-lights upon the mysterious sides of Nature that we are less susceptible than of old to the thraldom of them. For my part, I rejoice that our age is one when the wisdom acquired by the wise is no longer " wisdom learnt with dread."

The Grotto of the Cumean Sibyl, linked by mythological tradition to the nether world, is certainly one of the most impressive of all the features of this region. Following a little country road overgrown with grass and common flowers beneath the ruined Acropolis of Cumæ, pushing one's way through weeds and tangled greenery up to the tiny entrance overhung with trailing boughs, one is scarcely prepared for the weird grandeur of the cavernous depths within. Surely no more striking embodiment of the myth of the descent into Hades can be found in Nature : the contrast from the gorgeous sunshine to the monstrous damp shadows of this giant vault may have something to do with the profound

## ON A HOUSE TOP, SORRENTO

A few among the old women still spin with Homeric
simplicity.

sensation produced by the sudden plunge from light into mysterious gloom. Imagine a vast tunnel of crumbling stone, lofty as the main aisle of some Gothic cathedral which the ages had rudely shattered. Running along for a space, a lower tunnel continues the way; and far above may be seen a second story, or rather where once an upper floor existed. Through the narrow passage we again reach a wider space, and so on, indefinitely, until the road sinks into semi-darkness, and, almost overpowered by the sensation of heavy blackness all around, we pause and half wonder whether indeed the toils of the nether world are not really at hand to engulf us. Occasionally narrow slits in the rock far above let a faint glimmer of dusty light reach us, and now and then we come upon extraordinary flights of stairs and shattered remnants of the hundred portals. The effect is worthy of the imagination of a Gustave Doré in some inspired moment. What other spot could have created the grand picture in the *Æneid* of the frenzied Sibyl in her wind-swept abode? How the dark, shadowy walls seem impregnated with vatic utterances! while the dim path seems surely to descend to Stygian waters.

Out we come at last into the kindly sunshine. We rub our eyes, and the gloom of a moment ago sinks back into the impossible past. But we realise more clearly and fully that we are in the midst of the land of Homer, on the ground which answers so perfectly as the boundary of the living world and the confines of the infernal regions. Yet this Grotto of the Sibyl was once, according to the earliest Christian author who, after Virgil's time, mentions the Cumean Oracle, as highly polished and as richly beautiful as a basilica. We have seen but the shell, empty now save for the mystery which still fills it.

Besides the tombs found lately in the neighbourhood of Cumæ, which are thought to be purely Hellenic, an object of quite especial interest was found here not very long ago. Mr. Stevens came upon a tomb containing a tortoise-shell disc, a unique object which experts believe to have served as a polished mirror. No tortoise-shell of ancient days has ever been discovered before. Indeed not, I believe, until quite well into the Middle Ages have any objects made of it come down to us. Its whole history is obscure, nor do Pliny's remarks enlighten us very much.

We are now in the very midst of the great craters of the Phlegrean fields, known to the early navigators as the land of the Round Eyes. They stretch along the whole route from Naples to Cumæ, some rising above us, others sinking into hollow lakes. The brilliant if fantastic writer who has lately published in France a delightful work on this coast [1] has instilled quite a fresh interest into the Homeric land by his new and plausible theories. Boldly putting aside the accepted conclusions of the last century that the two great poems of the *Iliad* and the *Odyssey* were the creations of several poets who had gathered their materials from the same cycle of legends, Monsieur Bérard gives his reasons for believing

---

[1] *Les Phéniciens et l'Odyssée*, by Victor Bérard.

RUINED CASTLE OF LATTERE ON THE
HILLS ABOVE GRAGNANO

The hill crowned by this splendid ruin overlooks the
entire plain of Pompeii.

that the Greek Homer was the sole author, while
Odysseus, the great navigator, was himself a Phenician.
For the Greeks, he argues, travelled but little in those
days, a thousand years before Christ, while the Phenicians
were of course the great sailors of the world, spreading the stories and legends of their birthplace to far-off
lands, and thus providing the vast material from which
Homeric descriptions are drawn. The idea that the
Greek mind could be so exquisitely visionary as to blend
into their great legends purely imaginative and almost
fantastic scenery, is contrary to his conception of their
character, and is a view (he thinks) detracting from the
value of the poems, which can be fully understood only
by those who, accepting the Homeric geography as exact
in every detail, realise that since the days of antiquity
the mariner's route is still all unchanged, and that the
names and terms through which the Odyssean voyage
has been transmitted to us are in sense identical still.

To illustrate this view, Monsieur Bérard traces
Phenician roots in the Greek names lingering round the
Italian coast from Capri to Antium. In the Cape of
the Vulture, between Cumæ and Gaeta, he finds the
secret of the genealogy of Circe, daughter of Kyrkos, a
bird sacred to Apollo, and of Perse, a word which in
Greek would have no apparent meaning, but in Semitic
signifies a bird of prey and has been translated "eagle
of the sea." Then, again, the strange drug, "Moly,"
which Hermes gave to Odysseus, black at its root and
with a flower like milk, and so hard to uproot that only
the Gods succeeded, has itself a Semitic name which

translates into the *Atriplex halinum* peculiar to the Mediterranean coasts and probably unknown to Greece. Its flower is pale, the root clinging and difficult to unearth. Monsieur Bérard tried in vain to pull up even the smallest of its roots. " Les dieux seuls, qui peuvent tout, en sont capables."

But the writer's comparison of the " floating isle " with the island of Stromboli, because the latter threw up masses of débris from its crater, which floated about the seas, seems somewhat fantastic.

Though the idea that this land genuinely stimulated the descriptions in Homer is not by any means a new one, I believe that Monsieur Bérard is the first to find a connection between its peculiar features and the characters themselves in the *Odyssey*. The links between the strange physiognomy of this country and its equally strange names are most entertaining. Inland we see the extinct crater of the Solfatara, which is as the round eye of the Cyclops, from the lids and eyebrows of which the vapour of the burning pupil mounted. Then, too, not far off may be seen Mount Gaurus, a transcription in Greek of the Semitic word signifying blind. The Gaurus was the blind eye !

The whole scenery is dotted with round eyes like a photograph of the moon—eyes, long blind, that once must have flashed with living fire ! These extinct ruins of Nature are in keeping with the almost defiant works of the Roman decadence which for a brief period amazed the world. While the rude forces of the lower world held their own inland, the Romans ever behaved as if

HOUSE OF THE FAUN, POMPEII

they intended to hold the ravaging of the sea for all
time in check. Harbours, temples, gigantic fishponds,
and magnificent villas rose (as it were) from the very
water and defied the waves. They were buildings that
mocked at all sense of repose, and their very ruins still
inspire us with a curious unrest.

Perhaps the loveliest bit of Nature about the winding
road is found on the way to Baiæ. Through the sunny
vineyards, past the green-clad coasts, we look down into
the blue sea where the rose petals were once scattered
at the great Roman festivals as if gently to persuade it
to keep its many secrets. On one side of us lies the
little dead sea, and on the other the port of Misena,
while beyond stretches the low sandy beach to Gaeta.
Or turning from the coast, we reach the long, shallow
stretch of water of the Lake of Fusaro. Here, in the
little osteria overlooking the lake, we stopped for a
hurried meal under the shade of the trees. The oysters
may have lost their classic flavour, but they are still
fresh. Large or small, highly flavoured or not, the
oyster is the queen among shellfish. "Le poisson est
fin," as I once remember a *maître d'hôtel* saying with
real enthusiasm in Paris ; "mais l'huître est fine."
Untranslatable nuance ! A white wine, with a sourness
far from peculiar to wines of these parts of Italy, is
offered with the oysters.

The little inn is kept by a family literally hung over
with charms against the evil eye. For years the padrone
had boasted of his fine health and physique without
having recourse to their protective charm ; but the day

came when a severe illness made him bitterly regret his want of tact, and he now seeks to make up for past negligence by the wearing of the biggest horn that could be found.

We wandered through the pretty and now wild grounds, and found them full of the *tristesse* of neglect. Great palm-trees, parched with the sun of June, were dying in their beds ; flowers trailed over the paths and were crushed underfoot. All looked utterly deserted, and the Pavilion rising out of the transparent lake was more like a mirage of past years than anything tangible. But the air—how sweet and fresh it was ! What temptation to linger there and forget the shadeless road and the little dusty white vehicles awaiting us ! In all this country spots like this strike one as a species of oasis in a hot volcanic expanse. This sightseeing about the Phlegrean fields is ever an exhausting excursion crushed into one day, leaving on the mind a most confusing impression of heat and shadelessness, of dormant nature, of vistas of living beauty, and of irritating struggles with guides, cabs, beggars, and distances ; until in the cool evening we are finally driven back by the swift little horses, " fins, diligents, malins et plein de feu," as an eighteenth-century writer described their race,—back into the appalling noise of Naples, through which we can no longer hear

> " . . . like ocean on a western beach
> The surge and thunder of the Odyssey."

If we go back by the Fuorigrotta road we pass the turn

## HOUSE OF THE DRUNKEN FAUN, POMPEII

An attempt has been made of late to plant gardens
decorating the peristilium with flowers as of old.

which leads to the far-off Camaldoli, the most exquisite of all the environs of Naples. Its sixteenth-century monastery was built for the Camaldulian order, one of the lesser in importance of the monastic eleventh-century communities. The Camaldulian rule was that of S. Benedict, and their buildings were never built nearer than five leagues from a city, while they sought solitary and often barren heights to congregate on. But this spot is thickly clad with trees to the very gates of the monastery, and the air blowing about it is sweet and scented. Lucky are those who are able to make this charming excursion and picnic on the garden terrace of the Veduta Pagliana, from which a splendid view may be had.

The monastery itself is entered through a lovely cloister, at the end of which stands a quaint shrine, a medley of strange once-gaudy colours toned by time into harmony. After passing a door on the right, the spacious garden is reached, and a glimpse is obtained of the lonely monastic life led by the ten fathers who linger here. Each monk has a tiny cabin, built of white plaster and roofed with light red tiles, and about each cabin is a small garden of vegetables which the occupant cultivates himself, since this is part of the prescribed routine of life. Beyond is a lovely terrace which over-looks the whole bay of Baiæ and embraces a panorama of the entire coast.

A chat with one of the fathers gave an idea of the peaceful atmosphere which is theirs. " When I was a young man," said he, " I had a great enthusiasm for painting, and intended to devote my life to it. I studied in the Academy of S. Luke, in Rome, until, at the age of about thirty, the desire seized me to enter the cloistered life. Since then I have lived in this spot, and I scarcely ever hear from my old friends and relations or from the outer world."

"Do you never regret the sacrifice of all your artistic ambitions ?"

"No," he said : "I am supremely happy here, and would not alter my life in any way."

Certainly, standing in the shade of the widespreading trees on the verge of the beautiful terrace, and watching the sun sink like a globe of fire into the distant expanse so far beneath one's feet, we feel the restful spirit of the Lotus-eater envelop us,

"On the hills like Gods together
Careless of mankind."

But even here the breath of a Pagan land is taking possession of us.

Must there not have existed, in those dark ages when the monastic life grew into such especial favour, some hidden vein of the sentiment of the beauty of landscape among its followers, some cult of the Beautiful quite as real in its way as anything of our own times ?

HOUSE OF OLCONIUS, POMPEII

# CHAPTER VI

## FROM NAPLES TO CASTELLAMARE

ONE hot day early in June we drove from Naples to Castellamare. The heat and the dust seemed to be more bearable in an open carriage than in the hot compartment of the railway train. It is wiser, too, not to trust implicitly in this oldest train service in Italy. It should be treated as an interesting but antique relic of the days of Ferdinand II., who opened the line by travelling with the Queen in a splendid royal car lined with red damask and uncovered. The last time we travelled on this line the engine broke down completely, and, unlike the proverbial three-legged horse of Naples, had to be tugged instead of driven to its goal.

In spite of jolting roads and indescribable noise, the kaleidoscopic scenery of the towns on the way is rich in human interest and variety. On this particular day the Festa of Monte Vergine was drawing to a close, and hundreds and hundreds of pilgrim-laden carriages—victorias, bagarini, brakes, and char-à-bancs—tore past us at an inconceivable rate. Most of the drivers were running races regardlessly of any one's safety, lashing their wretched horses, and addressing them with untold insolence. The jingling and gleaming of fantastic trappings, the noise and the appalling dust, were enough, as they once said, to rouse the dead under the pavement in the Church of S. Anna.[1]

The singing and shouting of the pilgrims, and the waving of their long poles hung with dancing ribbons and souvenirs, made a wild and nerve-breaking scene. Our own horses took to the same breakneck pace. "Piano, piano," we cried. "Think of your poor horses."

"Non avra paura, signore. They are accustomed to the whip. I am not one of those who ill-treat their beasts. I treat them far better than I do my wife." With this consoling information, we dashed on into the mad cavalcade pouring towards us on either side.

The whole scene, brilliant though it be with colour and life, is too utterly reckless to impress foreigners agreeably. All Neapolitan festivals have a singular mixture of childish enjoyment and racy disregard of life and safety in general, and what with mad driving and excited tempers these great occasions never end without tragedy of some kind.

It seems to be the smart thing in this *fête* for the men to make up parties of four, and to dress themselves and the driver in clothes of the same colour, with hat and gaudy necktie exactly alike. Many of these

[1] The ugly Church of S. Anna, which contained the marvellous statue of the saint, to whom the fisher-folk all over Naples once prayed, was burned down in 1885.

THE VILLA CRAWFORD

As seen from the grounds of Il Pizzo.

turn-outs passed us, most of them in grays and fawns to dissimulate some of the dust ; but on this third day men and women were all alike, so thickly powdered with it that clothes, hair, and face were perfectly gray, presenting a truly ghastly appearance. The heat, too, was great, and the dust had changed to paste on many hot faces. The women make the pilgrimage hatless ; but the well-to-do have fastened to their vehicles basket trunks containing two changes of costume, since the real *luxe* of this extraordinary *fête* obliges a new toilette, each more gorgeous than the other, on the three successive days. Both men and women make elaborate preparations and ablutions for the occasion, washing all traces of oil or pomade from the hair, since grease in any form is disagreeable to the Madonna. Nor must greasy substances, such as bacon or loin of veal, be carried up the mountain-side in the luncheon baskets or in the pockets of the pilgrims ; and those who would feast on sausages and the oily food dear to the Neapolitan, must consume it at the foot of the ascent.

It would be interesting, as an Italian writer points out, to discover the origin of mountain heights for the Madonna's shrine, and the reason why her Son chooses ever the plain in which to erect His House, spots easy of access and within reach of all modern conveyances. In this particular instance the mountain height as a shrine dates back to classic times, since this church of Montevergine covers the site of a temple to Cybele, the mother of the gods.

# Naples

With a sense of relief, we gradually left the throngs of hunted horses and unrecognisable occupants behind, and rattled along through S. Iorio, which lies about half-way between Naples and Portici, and was once a favourite summer resort of the Neapolitans. The gardens of the palaces then stretched right down to the sea ; but long ago the railway ruthlessly divided them. Instead of the perfume of flowers, an overpowering odour of tanyards fills the air. But as we pass along the hot and dusty high road with the tram-line following it, vistas of gardens and of orange groves are seen through the open doors and courtyards of the houses.

Portici is dirty and uninteresting. Its tall houses look old and dark, and it is difficult to imagine the place even as it was in the days of the Bourbons, who did so much for it. What with factories of every kind, the royal buildings which sprang up under their rule are sold or transformed, or about to change hands. The Villa Favourita, of so many eighteenth-century memories, is now divided into two dwellings, in private hands. It was in 1768 that it was first opened with a splendid *fête* in honour of Marie Caroline—a *fête* at which the Emperor of Austria himself was present. When, soon afterwards, it became the property of the King, it was known as the "Favourita," to remind the Queen, perhaps, of the imperial villa of that name at Schönbrunn.

The beautiful Pauline Bonaparte stayed here in 1814, when her brother was prisoner at Elba. But

EVENING NEAR MASSA, PENINSULA OF
SORRENTO

charming as was the villa and its lovely grounds, its position, directly beneath Vesuvius, was a somewhat strange choice for those days, when eruptions of a serious nature were not infrequent. Lady Morgan describes in her *Italie* how the lava seemed literally to enter the very windows !

It was in this villa, in 1879, that the unfortunate Ismail was allowed to take up his residence, and the entire building was reconstructed to suit him and his harem. All kinds of legends sprang up of the wild and oriental luxury of his life. The courtyard was said to be strewn with sand imported from the desert and still hot with the African sun ! Yet his harem consisted of only three wives, and far from living in contented happiness during his seven years' seclusion there, Ismail was probably counting the hours until he could regain his kingdom and leave his exile for ever.

I am told that it is intended to erect a Colonial Museum, with Zoological Gardens, in the Palace of Portici. That is a project of the Duca d' Andria, who is well known for his interest in public works. Were it carried out, it might instil a new life into the town.

This palace was built in 1738, the year after the terrible eruption had destroyed so much in Portici and Torre del Greco. No town displays a history of more temerity than Portici in its defiance of menacing danger. When the young King was warned that he was choosing a strangely unsafe spot for his "Fontainebleau," his answer showed that he had already digested the favourite phrase of his new people : " Iddio, Maria Immaculata, e San

Gennaro, ci ponseranno!" So built it was; and ten years later his son, the worthless Ferdinand, was born in it.

Down by the shore all is busy, dirty, and over-crowded, but truly characteristic of old Portici. It is the "Granatielle" of which the popular cherry song says—

"I made love to a Portici maid
In the time of the cherries last year—
In the Granatielle, where the sea flows
Lived Rose—Rose the fair, they said.
O sweet time of tears and embraces;
As large as a cherry each tear,
Each kiss as sweet as a rose!
Cherries! Cherries!" [1]

It is but three or four hours' drive from Naples to Castellamare; yet we pass through five towns on the way. Resina, as all know, stands above Herculaneum, the first victim of Vesuvius. Under the dirty little town lie the silent homes of past generations which, so a German writer affirmed, were built upon a bed of tufa, precisely like that which destroyed them. It is now a veritable tomb, from which each year the tourists break away some fragments of marble skeleton. The sweet air blows through the Pompeian town, filling it with life; but here the damp odour of earth, the icy breath of marble, chills one on the warmest summer day, and is redolent of death. The excavations remain much as they were a century ago, and all that will ever be known of Herculaneum seems already known.

[1] Free translation for the Neapolitan 'E Cerase di Giacomo.

OLD GARDEN GATEWAY, SORRENTO

# From Naples to Castellamare

Torre del Greco is far the most beautiful of the towns along this road. Here, soon after the noise and excitement of Montevergine have subsided, begins the Festa of the Quatro Altare. Preparations for it were going on in the streets as we passed through the town. Altars were being erected and decorated with curious pieces of rough coral. In front of each altar would be spread a beautiful carpet of green moss and fresh flowers—a veritable mosaic of Bible designs. All the labour for the decorations of this Festa is voluntary. Poor workmen give gladly their spare time for weeks beforehand to build and ornament the altars, counting their labour well spent, though all the flower work of infinite patience will be destroyed in a few minutes under the feet of the crowd who follow the Procession of the Holy Sacrament, and the altars which have taken weeks of labour to erect are ruthlessly torn down the day after.

Many parts of this town are almost Oriental in appearance, and so richly picturesque as to outdo Naples in colour. The coral trade has bound the coast of Africa and Italy so closely at Torre del Greco that an undefinable Eastern quality is in the atmosphere. For centuries it has been the principal and richest centre of the coral industry on this coast. No doubt it would have been richer still had there been more organisation and control among the fishermen of the eighteenth century ; but quarrels and difficulties were perpetually arising among them, and money and time wasted in disputes until Ferdinand IV. started a Consulate to regulate affairs. It was the Consulate's duty not only to settle all differences, but also to determine the opportune moments for departure to sea, with a view of lessening somewhat the many dangers of the coral trade—dangers terribly disproportionate to the risks run. It is curious to note in the old *codice Corallino* and in many of the old travellers' books of that time that the fishing-boats were always termed *felukas*, showing close contact with the East.

The story of coral is haunted with fanciful legends as well as great antiquity. There have been lapses of centuries between the rise and fall of its popularity as an ornament. In the golden age of the Greeks it reached a zenith in fashion; then, from 200 B.C. on towards the Middle Ages, it seems to have sunk entirely into the level of amulets. Not till the eighteenth century was it recognised as animal life; though as far back as the sixteenth it had been given a sex, the dark red being termed masculine. It was even believed that coral assumed a darker tint when worn by men, just as it is still said to grow pale when worn by any one in failing health. The difficulty of cutting it gave it a great value in the past; but this value has lessened with the decreasing taste for its use, and among the villages round the coast there are quite poor families who have quantities of valuable coral in their possession, for which they can now find no market. But its use as an amulet is not likely to die out easily, and many generations of peasant babies are no doubt destined to cut their teeth upon the old Latin symbol.

CAPRI

View taken from Massa through the olive groves.

# From Naples to Castellamare

Beyond "Annunziata," which Murat once vainly endeavoured to name after himself,—now interesting only as the point at which the train from Castellamare usually breaks down—the beautiful Pompeian plain stretches around. The strawberries were ripe behind the low walls, and we gathered some as we passed from the garden of a haggling old peasant. Between quiet fields, dotted with the bent figures of women-labourers, and the rose colour of their scattered dwellings, the white road winds smoothly — hardly whiter than the dust-covered vegetation on either side. Sky and sea are deep blue, and Vesuvius melts into the atmosphere like a vast Parma violet.

The island of Rovigliano, which has been but a dark spot hardly noticeable in the blue sea, grows now into clear fantastic shape, and the old tower of the sixteenth century rises from its black rock like a weird parasite. At one end, broken off from the island, stands a great pyramidical stone, which, seen from a certain point of view, somewhat resembles a mitred bishop swathed in a voluminous mantle of Roman fashion. The fisher-folk name it "S. Catello," the protective Saint of Stabiæ, and believe that those among them who pass the rock on certain days without reciting a particular oration are doomed to die within the year.

The island is coloured with legends of warlike and monastic times. Both fortress and convent, forms of dwelling which in the Middle Ages were invariably associated with the darker side of history, have risen from it. In 1860 the State sold it to a private owner

who turned it into a summer pleasure-ground, as far
as wave-washed rock and ruined tower would allow
of such transformation.

In spite of the ceaseless Festas and the eternal
business of hanging up or pulling down coloured
lamps and flags and gaudy decorations, the town of
Castellamare is uninteresting. All festivals in the
South are precisely the same—made up of fireworks,
a band, and best clothes in which their wearers are
wretched. The women of the country wear all their
jewelry on these great occasions, often displaying quite a
quantity, for the Italian invests his money in gems that
he can count and look after instead of putting his
faith in any bank. In Naples, on the contrary, it is
rare to see women of any class out of doors with jewelry
on ; it would be stolen without loss of time.

Impossible to enter Castellamare on any day of the
year that some festival is not in course of creation or
of destruction. One asks oneself how often the same
red, blue, and green flags and rags, hitched up and
down from window to window, will continue to delight
the souls of this crowd, who seem to have nothing to
do but look on at the day's preparations, or listen all
night to the preposterous noise of fireworks. How
often during the last summer have we listened to their
spluttering fire across the bay, while Vesuvius was
uttering thunderous low roars, and a brilliant river
of crimson fire ran half-way down its sides towards
the moonlit sea !

This love of pleasure, combined with the exciting

STREET SCENE IN SORRENTO

fireworks, seems to have made this one of the most quarrelsome towns round Naples. The men are socialistic and disorderly, and the women fight tooth and nail up those dark side streets which are more lively in every way than pleasant. So, what with noise and the odour of crushed beetles peculiar to its streets, it is with real delight that we reach the beautiful ascent to Quisisana, up which the air sweetens and the blue of the sea grows deeper between the trees. Here we are in a veritable garden of greenery, chestnuts, olives, stone pines, and flowers! Beautiful villas spread up the hill; houses of Pompeian red show between the trees; little alcoves painted bright blue like the china shrines of the Della Robbias ornament the peasants' homes; and up and on winds the once royal park of the Villa Margherita—up into the heights where Robert of Anjou, cured of what seemed an incurable illness, planted a wood in his gratitude. Beyond a dark avenue gleams the villa itself, red as a sunset. Is it purely imagination, or does something royal still hover about it? Impossible to wander through deserted gardens, through silent rooms, without conjuring up the human elements that once inspired them all. A whole gallery of foreign portraits of sickly kings, in search of medicinal springs and dry fresh air, rises before the mind's eye, flitting like living ghosts about the place. At what date the charming name of Quisisana was first given to the villa we know not for certain; but I imagine that it was not later than the time of the Anjous, and the

# Naples

Bourbons did little more than revive it. The following verses on Quisisana, written in the early part of the seventeenth century, speak of the title as already of the past : —

> "The lofty shrines, grand deeds of Frankish reign,
> I saw upon one side, and far away
> The entrance above which was once inscribed,
> 'Here life is saved, and health ye may regain.'
> How much since then, I mused, of human pride,
> Of structure masterly in strength that once
> Rose proudly and robustly from our earth,
> Before great Time's voracity has died.
> Wistfully musing on these things, above
> A face looked down—so fair, it ravished me.
> 'Ah me,' I cried, 'what miracle is this,
> Amidst these ruins what hidden treasure of Love ?'
> More wondrous still, I who would restore
> My soul—where all find health, now breathe no more." [1]

It is now the Bourbon element which lingers most perceptibly about this solitary villa. The avenues, the fine roads, the great terrace with its superb view, are theirs. Here Ferdinand came with his brilliant wife—"le roi Caroline," as she styled herself—in those idle summer days when it was too hot "to shoot at the birds, dance with the girls, and eat macaroni." And we can imagine that the lovely Lady Hamilton, herself like some bacchante of the past, may have wandered with the Queen through the glades. But the fountains that played then under the shade of the

[1] Translated from the Neapolitan of Dottor Dominico de Santis. Naples, 1633.

IN THE GROUNDS OF MARION
CRAWFORD'S VILLA

# From Naples to Castellamare

trees are now silent, and the steps leading up to them are overgrown with moss.

Let us step out for a moment on the great terrace beneath which such a magnificent view lies spread. From this height Vesuvius exhibits perhaps its finest aspect from this side of the bay. It has a noble sweep across the curve of land, and the spirals of smoke curl far out to sea. Strange that the peaceful character of Vesuvius should have attracted so little artistic attention in the past! I know of no attempt ever made, even a century ago, to figure the mountain dormant. The famous picture by Wright, painted at the end of the eighteenth century, was but one among hundreds of efforts to depict it as "awful beyond description."

In all this view Castellamare includes one rare charm which is denied to many a lovely town along the coast. It enjoys the full view of the setting sun, which dips down into the water across its bay. Night after night in summer the great globe of fire is washed away before our eyes, and long after it has sunk below the sea the afterglow clings round the horizon like some ineffaceable stain. Far away the island of Capri— "that huge mound of rock which gathers out of the sky hues softer than the violet"—sinks into purple mist. Gradually, as the light fades, and the belt of towns around the coast—its string of pearls—grows dim, little lights begin to flicker near the water, and a necklace of gold gleams in its stead.

The first impression of Castellamare is one of perpetual spring. The last, if we linger long enough to find it, is rather one of impalpable age, which blends something of unreality into the surrounding nature. In spite of the language of this year's season, the world, as Norway says in his charming book, seems older here than elsewhere—older, perhaps, because its historic past is shattered as well as buried. A date, a fact, a stone, and the past becomes part of the life we know; but Stabiæ is still the tomb of only legends.

The spirit of excavation is surely one of the most remarkable characteristics of our day—"the making hue and cry after many a city that has run away, and by certain marks and token, pursuing to find it." Within a few years Herculaneum, Pompeii, Stabiæ, and Pæstum were "discovered"; and what a curious renaissance of learning and research was opened with this spade-digging in the south of Italy, where, till then, the Italians had been as naturally builders above ruins as we have now become delvers beneath the soil! Building above tombs marked with them passionate attachment to the spot, as may be traced in the history of the Stabiæns. Like human ants, they returned to reconstruct dwellings out of ruins, to-day out of yesterday; and the French traveller of the eighteenth century who attributed their persevering spirit to the utter blindness and folly of the human race, failed to grasp the peculiar atmosphere of this beautiful country and the Greek love of birthplace which lingers still among its inhabitants.

On the heights of Quisisana we are in the Faubourg of all that buried past, and the air that blows from

PORTRAIT OF TARANTELLA DANCER
WITH CASTANETS

# From Naples to Castellamare

Mont Angelo to the sea, is still as pure as in the days when it was sought as a haven of health by the Romans. An atmosphere of classic and royal convalescence from ancient days down to Tiberius, and on from the time of the Anjous, seems still to linger about the place. We can see the whole plain where the great tragedy of 79 was enacted; mark the spots where, dotted like a milky way, white with colonnaded villas, and temples to Minerva, to Hercules, to Diana and Ceres, lay the doomed cities of the Campania; conjecture the flight from Pompeii towards the sea, and along the Stabiæn road to the height where we stand, and so to Sorrento. But, wonderful as it was, perhaps it was not more so than the scene left behind, when a gray desert of lava and pumice stones stretched from the mountain to Castellamare, and amidst that desolation a relief party landed on the shore beneath, to search for the body of the brave old admiral. The name of Pliny reminds us that in the summer of 1899 there were some excavations that seemed to throw a new light upon his death—light obviously illusive when compared with the precious details left to us in the *Letters of Pliny* the younger.

"In July 1899 certain desultory excavations were undertaken on the farm of Signor Matrone, between the river Sarno and the Stabiæn gate of Pompeii, near the Molino Fienzo, not for any archæological or scientific purpose, but in quest of valuables and marketable objects. The results brought to light include a set of shops, built in the reticulated style, opening into a porch or veranda which runs parallel with the high road.　One belonged to a wine-seller, a second to a carpenter, a third to a dealer in fishing implements.　A large court opens behind the shops with an oven in the middle.　The place, in short, shows the characteristics of a country inn located on the Via Stabiai, near the mouth of the Sarno, on the main line of retreat of the panic-stricken Pompeians.　Seventy or eighty fugitives were found apparently smothered while seeking shelter under the roof of the inn, almost in view of the fleet from Misena coming to their rescue.　The greatest number fell at the east end of the porch towards the river, where Pliny's *Liburna* was probably anchored—a poor and wretched lot of fugitives, carrying away in their flight only a few coppers.

"Six or seven skeletons were found lying in the court near the oven—also with no objects of value.　But a party of men and women and children of much higher rank were overtaken by death in the middle section of the veranda.　Their gold necklaces were still fastened round their necks ; bracelets still encircled their wrists ; precious rings still fitted to their fingers.

"Among this group of well-to-do fugitives one seemed to occupy the place of honour, a person whose skull betrays a superior intelligence, and of a noble demeanour. He wore a chain of sixty-four gold rings wound thrice round the neck, two armillæ on the right arm, a heavy signet ring, and a dagger on the left side.　This dagger has a blade of steel.　This person was suffocated by the deadly fumes of the volcano while sitting against the wall.

THE VILLA CRAWFORD, SORRENTO

Early spring, wistaria in full flower.

# From Naples to Castellamare

"Excavations were carried on carelessly and no photos taken. In 1901 Signor Mariano Canizzaro, in a paper printed for private circulation, suggested that the skeleton might be that of Pliny the elder himself. The skeleton was found surrounded by a vast quantity of household gods and goods, such as tripods, some modelled in terra-cotta. Unless these objects belonged to Pompeians (in whose company Pliny probably was at the time of the catastrophe), we cannot imagine that the gallant old admiral was rushing to the rescue of the Pompeians and Herculaneans with a lot of clay figures in his hands."[1]

Except for the treasures of sculptured and inscribed fragments buried in the dusty vaults of the cathedral, nothing older than mediæval times is to be seen about Castellamare. Before the Church of Pozzano, in a solitary corner, overlooking the water, a cross rises from a fluted column poised upon a marble altar to Diana, a tiny relic of those Pagan days that has outlasted temples and monuments. The emblem of the Goddess, a garlanded stag, is sculptured on either side, and round the pedestal are exquisite wreaths of flowers and fruit. The rose-tipped marble is dented and dulled now, the toy of the idly busy hands of children.

Below it juts out the old castle of the Middle Ages from which Castellamare is said to have derived its name.

Mediæval times changed the character of this coast as completely as Christianity and its Churches wiped away the traces of Paganism. Towers and castles gave

[1] R. Lanciani.

117

a warlike appearance to the soft outlines of the rocks
above the sea. They spoke of conflicting races, foreign
influences, a harder struggle for power. The sea and
the land, the mountain and the plain, were at war with
each other, and strongholds watched the water and
campania with distrustful eye. Those days were
comparatively but of yesterday ; yet they sometimes
seem to lie far beyond the Greco-Roman days with
which we are in touch in thought and art. The purely
fighting spirit is hard to transmit from one age to
another ; and the ruined and moss-covered castles of
the Middle Ages belong more entirely to the past than
many a temple now open to the sky. But this castle
of the sea, standing pale and gray amidst the green-grays
of the olives about it, with the snow-white butterflies
of summer fluttering beneath its walls, speaks of more
than the mere strength of stone above stone, of more
than the stern struggle of foreign races and their decay.
About it hovers the great name of him whose life is
summed up in the words, "Stupor Mundi," the greatest
of all mediæval characters. Though Frederick loved
best the Apulian coast and left there the memories of
his life and too early death, a thread of the learning
and culture which has long outlived his wars encircled
the shining bay from Naples to Salerno ; and if the
chains of that time, the superstitions, the astrological
fables which then flooded the world, sometimes held
him bound, how natural does all belief in hidden powers
seem around this coast, where the voices of the lower
as well as of the upper world are ever murmuring !

ON THE ROAD TO MASSA

The popular evening drive from Sorrento in the
summer months.

# From Naples to Castellamare

So they are mediæval times which speak in the very name of Castellamare, and all the older past is undefined; yet it is a "past which is always present." There is hardly a ruin now in the light of day to speak of it; but its echoes linger among the classic hills above, which have watched the eternal changes of that mountain across the water which the ancients believed changeless.

Among the many beautiful excursions round Castellamare is the drive to the Castle of Lettere, of which little is known, though it is a landmark of evident importance in its time. To reach it we drive through Gragnano, whose long street seems to wind for over a mile before it opens into the country road. Though this town is within easy reach of Castellamare and the properties of Neapolitan families lie around, there is something quite distinct and of the past about its life. The art of spinning is still to be seen, old women sitting at their doors distaff in hand. What woman's work can compare with it in grace? Was this the reason why in ancient times, when fair ladies spun for their pleasure, a stern rural law forbade its use out of doors?

A strong smell of uncooked macaroni fills the air; the house doors and even windows are hung with the lemon-tinted *spaghetti*—or twine, as it is called. In drying it deepens to orange colour, and hangs hard and stiff. It is spread side by side with the drying clothes, and in and out among the stands of gold fringe goes on all the street life of the inhabitants. Women are having their hair dressed; little girls are busy winding thread and wool off revolving wheels; old women with their distaffs, cobblers toiling with bent shoulders, and crowds of screaming and laughing children are on every side. If it were not for one thing all would be pleasant enough to look upon ; but old and young, plain and good-looking, are afflicted with goître. Terrible and disfiguring illness ! There is now a French remedy for goître in its early stages ; but the boon of modern progress, of modern hygiene, is all unknown in these poor villages, where the same modes of suffering are passed on like heirlooms, from one generation to another. I am told that the disease in Gragnano and in Pimonte, a little higher up, is as old as its history.

Our carriage was pursued through the long street by a crowd of begging children, who had evidently received the most thoughtful attention from previous tourists. Getting none whatever from us, and very hoarse with yelling all in vain, one youth finally slung a stone into the carriage. This roused the sleeping lion. One of our party, who had chased other game across the South African veldt, sprang out, and down the street after the boy, who had taken to his heels like lightning. Every one was delighted. Faces appeared at the windows ; the cobblers grinned ; the macaroni-hangers beamed ; there was a delightful atmosphere of gratitude even for this small diversion. The boy received his punishment in the midst of an admiring audience, and we drove on through a crowd remarkable for its dignified reserve.

As we continued on the way the sound of women's voices chanting met us, and a procession of girls, from a few years old upwards, passed by, all with their hair

A GARDEN TERRACE, SORRENTO

combed out over their shoulders and floating in the air.
They were on their way to fetch the body of some young
companion, and to bear it to the grave. The procession
was led by the smallest child carrying a crucifix, upon
which they all kept their eyes fixed as they passed down
the street between the swaying gold of the macaroni,
chanting their monotonous prayer. How like is the
music of these parts to the wild droning of Egyptian
song! There is the same restriction of notes, the same
languor, the same sudden barbaric breaking of the voice.

The road to Gragnano is typical of all roads in this
country. Nowhere else are seen such mountains of white
dust. Everything on either side of the road for miles
becomes covered with it. A dark cypress is powdered
over until it is as pale as an olive. The aloes and
cactuses are almost white, and some of the trees remind
one at times of those in a child's Noah's ark encrusted
with snow. On a windless day it gives a fantastic,
quaintly beautiful effect. The shadows around are of
the purest azure. The road winds up the gorge, and
soon a bright campanile rises from the trees. Passing
through a village, we leave on the right the road to
Lettere, and keep straight on round the curve until the
great castle bursts upon the sight.

A grand old ruin of the Middle Ages this, of
Spanish and Aragon construction, with its frowning
central towers and battlemented walls. In a corner of
its chapel is a ruined fresco of the " Annunciation." It
stands above gentle slopes, all vine clad and wooded,
that lead down to the Campania, which lies like a blue

sea far below. The lines of the hills behind us seem to sink away into eternity. The whole castle is perched in a dreamy cloudland of its own.

> " Golden and rosy over it
> The clouds float dreamily."

There is a peculiar charm in the remains of mountainous feudal castles in this country, unnoticed elsewhere. The mountains around Naples are as bold in shape as are those of Scotland or of Germany, but infinitely softer and more luxuriant in colouring. There is upon their sternness a softening touch which seems to lift them into the sphere of the poetic and ideal.

CLOCK TOWER OF SORRENTO

# CHAPTER VII

## POMPEII

" Once more restored to the pure light of dawn
  After the vast oblivion of lost years,
  Back from the earth's voracious sepulchre
  The dead Pompeii's skeleton is drawn—
  —Back 'thwart the mournful ages and time's tears.
  And in the silent Forum, still and wide,
  Far beyond the shadows of the columns
  That, mutilated, lie on every side,
  Pilgrims may view the now divided mount
  About whose crest eternal vapours glide
  Still frowning exquisitely o'er our fears."
                    Translated from *La Ginestra*, Leopardi.

LEAVING the train at Annunziata, we drive past Pompeii itself towards the new centre of Madonna-worship, which has eclipsed in the last few years all others in its growth and wealth. A whole colony has sprung up about it. Prosperous schools have been founded ; trades are encouraged ; the poor are looked after. And all this is the work of a once poor and obscure notary. There is a saying in Italy that no Neapolitan lawyer can be honest. Whether this one in particular sought to disprove the proverb, I know not ; but he has made

123

for himself a name little less than miraculous. The extraordinary patience with which he saved up his humble earnings and carried out his ambitious scheme reads like a romance. The church itself is not large; but its luxurious ornamentation, rich interior, and purple lights, the sonorous roll of its superb organ, and the scent of incense which, unhampered by the close air of towns, rolls through the open door into the country street, impress the most callous visitor. On either side of the altar hang glittering golden offerings, souvenirs of whatever part of the poor human body has been cured of its ill. There is none of the dirt and squalor of so many church interiors of the South. All is new, gorgeous, intense, idolatrous. An atmosphere of devout and absorbing faith, of blind obeisance, is about the church. People are pouring in and out, none looking at each other, but all with eyes raised to the dazzling lights above the altar. Strange beyond words is this exotic growth of worship in the midst of an old Pagan plain, still haunted with the temples of the Gods, the tiny open-air and perfect sculpture of their altars.

The faith here is intensely human. All the vast sums of money subscribed from America and France and the richer parts of Italy are given in desperation. "Save me, my child, my husband, my parent, whoever it may be ; and all my earthly goods will I part with." Such is the spirit of this church, filled to overflowing with golden offerings, and with crippled and suffering bodies, and in an atmosphere suffocatingly sad. It is a

GARDEN OF THE PRINCESS
GORTCHAKOW'S VILLA AT SORRENTO

Famous for its beautiful palm trees.

joy to turn from it and to find some old and weather-beaten shrine in the pure air, before which the humble peasant kneels and mingles his prayers of the soul and the storm-driven heart. To the church the ills of the body are taken ; to the shrine the ills of the heart, confusing passionate and unbalanced love with the love of the pure and saintly. Here is a sunburnt labourer who leaves his cart and thin, ill-treated horse in the middle of the road, while he drags off his cap and falls on his knees before a painted image of the Madonna.

> "*Ave Maria !* She too bears thy name,
> She who has filled my poor heart with despair.
> Bitter are the tears she lets me shed,
> Infamy ! and little does she care !

> "*Full of Grace!* Thou knowest, Mother of love,
> That those who love as I forget no more.
> Give me this mark of thine especial favour,
> Into her heart some of these love's tears pour.

> "*Holy Mary !* When the night sets in,
> When I seek to close my heavy eyes,
> Fulfil this prayer . . . let me but fall to sleep.
> Never ! Mad am I otherwise.

> "*In this Hour !* . . . Oh, beautiful is she . . .
> But when she boasts that princes, noblemen,
> Would die for her as dies the setting sun. . . .
> *Our Death. Amen !* "[1]

A lady whose child was lying dangerously ill addressed all her fervent prayers to the Madonna of Pompeii. Praying long one day in her room, she heard

[1] Translation from the Neapolitan dialect of Sig. di Giacomo.

a loud clatter against the wall, as if the pots and pans in the neighbouring house had slipped off their nails. She sprang to her feet with joy. "It is the Madonna's voice answering me!" she cried. "I said, 'If the child recover, make me a sign, Holy Madonna'; and as I said the very words, came the answer." A devout Catholic told me the story, smiling—for among many such as he the Pompeian worship is not viewed with entire favour, the money speculation that keeps it going being well known.

As the amphitheatre of Pompeii lies near the road leading to the Church of the Madonna, let us wander into it before visiting the town itself. Whatever it was in the past, it is most beautiful now, covered by lovely grass slopes dotted with flowers and alive with butter-flies and lizards. Without indeed the grandeur that is found in such buildings elsewhere, or any great interest (save that its age is said to be greater than that of such permanent structures in Rome itself), there is a harmonious blending between its rough architecture and the natural formation of the site, for it is scooped out of the hollow of a hill—a large verdure-lined cup with circles of seats melting away into the smoothly sloping sides. It seems to have gathered about it an artificial poetry which certainly could not have existed about any amphitheatre in the past. The Roman amphitheatre never aimed at beauty of architecture—only at brutal solidity. Uninspired as the Romans were in this instance by the Greek spirit, they had nothing to work from but their own love

# Pompeii

of enduring masonry and solid display ; and the beauty
of this, among other amphitheatrical spots, is borrowed
from the lovely hills around and the purple distances
which so exquisitely envelop it.

In the newspapers of July 1862 appeared the
following absurd paragraph :—"At the moment of
the destruction of Pompeii by an eruption of Mount
Vesuvius, A.D. 79, a theatrical representation was
being given in the amphitheatre. A speculator
named Langini, taking advantage of that historical
reminiscence, has just constructed a theatre on the
ruins of Pompeii ; and the opening of which new
theatre he announces in the following terms :—'After
a lapse of 1800 years, the theatre of the city will be
reopened with *La Figlia del Reggimento*. I solicit
from the nobility and gentry a continuance of the
favour constantly bestowed on my predecessor, Marcus
Quintus Martius ; and beg to assure them that I
shall make every effort to equal the rare qualities
he displayed during his management.'" The scheme
proved beyond his ambitions.

Driving back along the dusty road, with the flat
green fields on either side, dotted with little painted
dwellings, we approach what seems in the distance to
be a mere settlement of mud huts. Whatever sentiments may be roused in some minds by the sight of
this ruined shell of tragically arrested life and pleasure,
it is impossible to shut one's eyes to the utter banality
of the tourist's visit. Arriving at what might be the
entrance of an Earl's Court exhibition (outside it is like

a great laundry yard, where the linen of the various hotels flaps about in the hot air), and having taken the tickets, and had an old and useless map of the city palmed off as new, the visitors anxiously inspect the guides, and try to decide which looks the least rapacious and the most bearable. "Get the fat guide—he is first-rate," we had often heard said ; but they were all fat, for the post of Pompeii is well known as a very nourishing one. Followed, then, by a guide, and armed with the map, which the tourist insists upon spreading out and studying with absorbed interest at every few steps, we enter the street of the dead city. Are those the voices of ghosts around, monotonous low voices, chanting in a sing-song tone from among the tiny ruins? No ; only the voices of fellow-tourists reading aloud their banal Baedekers in the enchanted ground. Here, on the left, we turn into the Temple of Apollo, one of the earliest of the excavated ruins. Casts of the original statues are poised on pedestals around, and upon them some half-dozen kodaks are turned, while a group of impatient guides wait at the gates. Now on towards the great Forum, where already in a corner sit a party with their luncheon basket empty before them, within a magic circle of orange peel and egg shells. Where is the poetry of it all ?

But there are other ways of seeing Pompeii than this joining in the great stream of foreigners. Take, for example, some day of *Festa* when the quaintly-dressed peasants from the mountains and the plains

FOUNTAIN IN SORRENTO

Typical of the many rose-coloured wall-fountains of
the South.

# Pompeii

around come for a day's sightseeing. The women are all decked out in gorgeous kerchiefs, their sunburnt faces and breeze-tossed hair bright with colour ; the men slouch along beside them, carrying the knotted handkerchiefs containing their humble meal. Many a handsome face is among them, many a dash of old-time beauty. They know nothing whatever of Pompeii ; but every moment of the day during which they tread clumsily on one another's heels over the still-polished stones is full of delight to them. Their rough laughter rings freely through the great Forum and the empty villas ; but it jars less on the ear than the more artificial pleasure of our own kind. The natives are a thousand times more in touch with the past amidst whose ruins they stand than the most profound archæologist of our time can ever be. They are the same people in spirit, in character, as their class was hundreds of years ago. They are lovers of pleasure, devoted to their soil, as poor and as hardy, as ignorant and as uncrushably hopeful as were the peasants of the happy plain about the once living city. Their homes are almost identical, rose-coloured, with sometimes a light wooden story above. They are still as paganistic in spirit as their religion will allow, or rather in spite of it, and their lives and homes are menaced by the same danger as that which hung over the Pompeians. How strange to feel about us in this spot a breath of the gay and still thoughtless life palpitating through it as of old ! What can the guides and guide-books tell us that is more living and true ?

# Naples

The actual impression produced by Pompeii as we see it to-day must be curiously opposite to the effect originally produced. We see a city of glaring sunshine, of shadeless streets, of almost uniformly low buildings, all penetrated with silence. There is hardly a corner where the sun is not now welcomed. But Pompeii was once full of deep shade. The very Forum must have had its awnings, and the narrowness of the thorough-fares was no doubt accentuated by the upper stories of the houses, which in many a tiny lane must have almost met overhead. There is hardly a street across which we could not easily jump ; but, owing to the fallen walls on either side, the public ways appear wider now. The houses were indeed, as a writer points out, constructed very much as birds construct their nests. The interiors of the dwellings, now so bright and sunny, were then softly darkened, while the air, which to-day penetrates so purely through their open and deserted recesses, must, unless methods of hygiene at that time were very well developed, have been little pleasanter or purer in that crowded centre of pleasure than in many a modern South Italian town. But Pompeii is now a model of swept and garnished care, which makes one feel at times as though it was entirely artificial, surrounded as it is by so many of the dirtiest little towns in the world.

The real sentiment of Pompeii seems to be little changed, whatever has happened to its outward appearance. It is indescribably gay and insouciant still, and the most sympathetic student would find it hard to be

BEACH OF THE FISHING VILLAGE OF
PUOLO

A short distance from Sorrento.

depressed here. Whether it is the site itself, or the moral atmosphere left by the people—who can tell?—it is the only ruin in the world over which the joy of life still hovers ; its streets are the only ones through which footsteps seem still to pass ; it is the one spot where life has left a complete vitality and a legend of joyfulness without the confusing changes of Time. I speak of joyousness in the Pagan sense, as it were—not to describe an existence more generally painless than ours, but a time during which the sufferings of others were certainly less considered and the Gods delighted in laughing at them. Life that could not be enjoyed was looked upon as a very worthless thing. The life of a slave must, therefore, have seemed peculiarly valueless : what did he know of the free happiness of living ? We in our time have reached so high a rung of civilisation that each man is burdened with the sorrows of humanity in general. His burden does not very sensibly lessen the misery of the world ; but it teaches him to know and to feel. Thus no doubt it is as much for himself as he is to-day constituted, as the lost art of viewing life was for the ancients.

The more one seeks to revive their day in the imagination, the more does the picture blend in with the climate and the peculiar character of the surrounding Nature. The Pompeians were a part of it, in harmony with it like some painting that only one frame can fit. We, as Taine says, wander from one city to another and find ourselves at home everywhere, and leave no Gods behind us.

# Naples

The life must have been strangely lazy! There could have been no traffic to speak of in the narrow streets. No trades were carried on in the town, no industries of any kind. All the labour of the town fell upon the slaves. There could not, therefore, have been any great *luxe*, since slave-labour would have proved insufficient to administer to it. They must have combined some secret of simplicity in their routine with their passion for luxury and pleasure, which would no doubt strike us as very comfortless. Certainly their homes give us no impression of being other than decorative asylums for the night or during bad weather.

Passing along the stone-worn streets, we look into the tiny shops, with their marble counters and sliding doors. In the counters are seen the holes where were balanced the amphoræ, so called from their ear-like handles on either side. They were the great oil, wine, and fruit jars which the Romans used as did the Greeks before them.

Beyond the Forum we see the small baths of Pompeii, the *Balneae* which constituted such a favourite luxury of that time, and in the perfecting of which our own day seems to have taught us little. Those for men and women were built side by side, so that one set of furnaces served for both, and the hot-water cisterns heated both alike. These baths must have been one of the most crowded and popular places in the town. The entrance fees were small, and children were admitted free. In the first room was performed the anointing with perfumed oil, which was afterwards scraped off by slaves

# Pompeii

with a sharp strigil. Slaves took charge of the garments when there was no dressing-room, as was sometimes the case in the smaller baths. In Pompeii may be seen the tiny niches where the clothes were laid while the bather went through all the luxurious processes of the Turkish bath, " killing " over the performance as many hours of the lazy day as he could.

There is no need, and it would be even out of place here, to describe the villas and buildings of Pompeii ; they are well known, and a hundred fascinating history-guides tell us their romantic story. But apart from all knowledge of details, there is a real charm in wandering through Pompeii and enjoying its beauty, which is so joyous and sunny. It seems to have gained with time. All that was tawdry and carelessly built has vanished. If the people of those days collected round them even a tenth of the useless and trivial objects that now make an excuse for the spending of money, no trace of them remains. Only what was purely decorative and artistic, or of real interest, has come down to us. Sometimes even these have been beautified. Look at the dancing faun in the house of that name ; what exquisite tints have coloured it ! It is bright with rust, the patina with which the ages have delighted in painting bronzes and coins. Dashes of blue and strange green gleam through the leaves of the little garden which of late years has been planted with an attempt at reviving the flower-gardens of the past. Tall poppies and sunflowers, roses and carnations and a trailing vine, fill the air with sweetness, and the spot seems but to await the musical play of a fountain to break the spell under which all sleeps.

Everywhere there are quantities of elf-like green lizards darting about as if continually searching for those lost races who looked upon them for so long as the creatures of good fortune instead of, as now, only fair game to catch by the slender tail. Their bite, according to Pliny (the inexhaustible Pliny), was fatal in Greece, but never in Italy. They were the type of divination, the symbol of Apollo, creatures of light and sight—an idea which is said to have arisen from the superstition that when the lizard grew old and blind it felt its way into the warm sunshine, and there recovered the use of its sight ; and Leland points out that Raphael painted his Madonna of the Lizard to illustrate the symbol of the blind turning towards the true Sun. A lizard with two tails is still considered a lucky find in some parts of Italy, and to many a wayfarer from the north the appearance of these bright and living jewels basking so joyfully in the warmth still gives an artistic delight which tempts one to view them as creatures not wholly devoid of their old tradition.

Another lovely garden is in the Casa dei Vettii, and here are a great wealth of charming frescoes. It is, of course, in these mural decorations that so much of Pompeian interest lies, though, alas ! they represented the art of but a few years, from the date of the first eruption in 63 to the year 79. These paintings of a decadent age in Rome and Pompeii form the chief source from which our knowledge of Greek painting is gathered.

OLIVE GROVE NEAR MASSA

In the autumn the peasants are seen gathering up the
olives and the firewood under the trees.

# Pompeii

Though mural decoration came to be regarded in the Republican period as of a very high rank, and the artists themselves often belonged to noble families, it was regarded in Pliny's time as belonging to a much lower plane of art, and the most famous artists painted only easel pictures, which have succumbed to the centuries. A large proportion of the wall paintings in Pompeii and on the Palatine are evidently the work of inferior craftsmen, and apart from their imperfect technique, they often exhibit an exaggerated taste in the subject as well—the sure portent of a growing decline. Vitruvius reprobated the custom of representing monsters instead of real objects, sham architecture instead of the simpler style of the time, and the too light and powerless supports for heavy entablatures which may be traced on the walls of Pompeii.

Certainly the inequality in the mural work is very noticeable in this little town. Some of the houses are decorated with designs exquisitely poetic, while others are as banal as second-rate wall-papers of to-day. But nothing has come down to us which can illustrate the level reached by painting ; and we can only imagine, as we view the graceful and bright decorations of the walls around us, on which the sunlight often falls now, what the great work of the richer towns, such as Neapolis and Capua, must have been like.

It is curious to note how small a part the colour blue plays in these frescoes. We know that it was one of the rarer and more expensive pigments, and from the rarity of it here one must conclude that the

Pompeians could not afford its constant use, or that they actually preferred the warmer tones of red and yellow. In the house of Ariadne is seen a corner once brilliant with the colour of the sky, but faded now. In the Museum of Naples are lumps of lapis-lazuli, which when powdered produced a sort of ultramarine tint ; but many of the lovelier and cheaper shades of blue drawn from copper soon blacken with exposure, and this fact no doubt influenced the choice of colours long ago.

Though so small in actual area, Pompeii can only be cursorily visited in a day. Many a visit is required before one can easily find one's way about its too-uniformly-laid-out streets, which at first sight look monotonously still and white. With the love of bright colour in this country, the outward pallor of Pompeii is all the more striking, and would certainly amaze the Pompeians themselves, who lived within and out of doors in a blaze of happy hues.

Having wandered through the town, we come to a hillside composed of three layers—cinders, small stones or *lapilli*, and fine white ashes, all soft and yielding to the spade. Beneath, in its cast of plaster of Paris, lies concealed the rest of the little town. Some hundred labourers, supervised by a director, are at work, and we may watch the progress of the enterprise, which will go on patiently for another half-century before the excavations are completed—two centuries in all to restore to the light this pleasure-spot of the past. Pompeii has, I believe, yielded less of late, though from the spurious

STREET OF POSITANO

imitations of bronzes, wall-paintings, and so on, which are quite openly sold by antiquity dealers as having *been stolen* from the town (for which reason they seem to find a ready market), one might imagine that Pompeii was an inexhaustible mine of treasure, and not, as is the case, a mine which was already largely despoiled before the centuries finally concealed it.

Still, one object of great importance was recently found here—a spirited statuette of Perseus, about twenty inches high ; a unique object, I believe, as far as ancient sculpture is concerned. All except weather-resisting finds are, of course, at once removed to the Museum, and as each gem is discovered and borne away, something of the life of Pompeii seems to go with it. Chateaubriand's dream was to see the objects in the place where they were found—to make of Pompeii the most perfect and living of museums instead of a despoiled tomb. That was indeed only a dream. Our age is an age of museums, invaluable but stifling.

Climbing the rough ascent to the fields above—which the peasants cultivate until, bit by bit, it is needed for the excavations,—we see the whole city spread out before us, while Vesuvius, less than a mile distant, rises beautifully above it. In the distance may be seen a moving line of ash- and earth-laden waggons crawling along towards the embankments which have gradually grown up round Pompeii, rendering it almost invisible from the plain. Near beneath us gleam the lately uncovered buildings, white and fresh. Beyond they have changed to smoke-colour, and beyond again to grimy black. Think ! Some of them have remained open to the sky and the elements for over a century and a half. The rain has beaten in ; the autumn winds have buffeted the ruined walls ; thousands upon thousands of tourists have scampered through them. What has been restored with infinite patience Time is once more steadily undermining, and with the ages Pompeii must crumble away beyond all power of resurrection. It is still the doomed city—unless for a third time Vesuvius should seek to immortalise it.

Far away inland lies Boscoreale, the seat of so many valuable finds of late years, which have now passed out of Italy into foreign museums. There was discovered the other day the house known as the Villa Pompeiana di P. Fannio Sinistore, said to be in many ways the most perfect and interesting yet excavated, and still more sumptuous than even that other villa so famous for the beautiful silver table service found in its cellar, which is now in the Musée du Louvre. It had a farm attached to it, though the rooms of the house itself were separate. A date affixed by a *graffito* on a column records a sale by auction, probably of the house itself, in A.D. 12. The whole plan of the building has been recovered, and offers, it is said, a good illustration of Vitruvius' statement that in pseudo-urban houses the peristyle often opened directly out of the vestibule. The wall decorations belong to the second or architectural style of Pompeian painting, and show some resemblance to the frescoes in the house of Livia on the Palatine.

# Pompeii

In regard to the magnificent frescoes found at
Boscoreale, an arrangement was made with the Government by which the owner on whose private ground
they were found should part with only a certain proportion of them to the country, while the rest were
exported to Paris, where Messrs. Canissa, antiquity
dealers of the Rue Lafayette, were to treat for their
purchase. The Berlin Museum made a splendid offer
for the lot; but the owner had, unfortunately for himself, exaggerated ideas of their market worth, considering them as far surpassing in value and interest anything
as yet found in or about Pompeii, and the offer was
refused. They were sold by auction a short time ago
for a much smaller sum. The Metropolitan Museum
of New York acquired the bulk of them, and among
others one of peculiar interest as illustrating the building
of the houses of that period, and showing the upper
stories of wood and the little balconies that jutted from
the windows, of which a single example may still be
traced in Pompeii to-day.

The Louvre purchased three of the frescoes, choosing
those which were of archæological interest rather than
those more remarkable for their beauty. Indeed, one
might almost infer from these three specimens, so poor
in colour and design, that they must have been chosen
with a view of also illustrating the bad painting of those
days which decorated the houses of the most wealthy!
One, depicting a genie holding in the left hand a
bowl, is certainly not of an inspired order of art, while
the more decorative friezes make one wonder at such

work penetrating the sumptuous dwelling in which they were found. Either the taste of the rich was not always *difficile*, or the history of painting in Pompeii itself may have been a short one, maturing as rapidly as its wines, and again declining as rapidly. No doubt, too, even then the advance of Christianity was beginning to undermine the mythology from which the artists drew their inspirations. The new religion may have had something to do with disturbing its expression, just as the mythological spirit itself penetrated for awhile into the paintings of holy subjects. New and uncertain elements must have been upsetting all the painting of that time, and this mingling of the known and the unknown has left us but a blurred mirror of the true fount of art and colour in which to gaze to-day.

AMALFI IN SUMMER

# CHAPTER VIII

## SORRENTO

"Laughing and happy spot!
Light-hearted and gay ;
If life hath moments of sorrow,
The blue sea takes them away,
Takes—and returns them not."
        DE CURTIS.   (Translated from the Neapolitan.)

THE drives to Sorrento, to Amalfi, to Salerno, may be considered as rivals in beauty, since the comparison of one lovely view of Nature with another seems indispensable to the modern traveller.  The drive from Castellamare to Sorrento, winding as it does between terraces of vineyards and orange groves, through the leaves of which the deep blue sea and sky and the violet slopes of Vesuvius are continually visible, is certainly one of the most beautiful in the world. Surely, while driving along this glittering road on an afternoon in late spring, it is impossible to imagine anything softer in atmosphere, or more dreamlike. The vegetation is wildly luxuriant.  There are green gorges, vine-clad overhanging rocks, sunny walls with

# Naples

enormous clumps of daisies above, and morning glories
and purple wistaria trailing over them all. The mingled
gold of the orange-trees where the fruit of the past
autumn still gleams among the blossoms of spring
follows the white and dusty road. Far beneath, washing over the shining rocks, the sea lies like a sapphire,
on which "a thousand rainbows have been thrown and
broken"; at moments a breeze sweeps over its surface
and darkens it to wine-colour—the very sea of the
*Odyssey*.

Every foot of ground that can be reclaimed on the
precipitous slopes is terraced and cultivated. Everywhere around us is the shimmering silver of the olive,
and often a lovely tracery of shadow is thrown upon the
road. Shadows are among the most subtle charms of the
South. In the North they are almost uniformly dark;
here they are but a transparent lacework, luminous and
variegated. Under the olives lies a purple tint as soft
as the wings of the dove; and the trembling vine-leaf,
eternally fanning itself, throws a shadow as cool as it is
pale. Paler still is the shade of the fig-tree, so light
that the tree can be planted with impunity among the
vineyards, as the ancients knew. As we pass between
the houses and walls by the way, a clear blue shade lies
across the road like a darkened heaven. Lovely and
full of poetry are these shadows of the South.

It was in the 'forties that this road was built by
Ferdinand the Second, and until now[1] no modern con-
trivances have broken into its exquisite remoteness.

[1] The electric tramway is to begin working this year.

AMALFI

From the terrace of the Cappucini Hotel. Autumn.

# Sorrento

No railway has whistled near ; no tramcar, electric or other, has rushed round its undulating curves. Only the slow-moving oxen, the patient mule, the small and rapid mountain horse, and those absurd teams which combine all three beasts, have beaten up the pumice dust in clouds along the road. Near Castellamare, in the gay summer season, the road is lined with light carriages and red-plumed horses waiting under the shade of the chestnut trees for the crowds of bathers on the shore. In spring and autumn tourist parties, with their luggage strapped on to their vehicles, pass continually to and fro between Naples and Salerno. The rate at which the horses fly past is unequalled for swiftness in any other country I know of. They whirl along, up hill and down, over the dust-white road between cliff and sea with a rapidity which would have horrified Dr. Johnson quite as much as the rolling gait of a stage coach delighted him. There is, too, a delightful sense of having found a faint element of old-time poetry of travel even along a path which, for the last sixty years, has been beaten by tourists of every kind. Honeymoon couples, for half a century, have loved it. Taine felt that where all was so beautiful " la vie peut redevenir simple comme au temps d'Homère."

Beautiful it must ever be ; but the road itself will lose one of its greatest charms with the opening tram-line. Its exquisite stillness will be broken into, and those who have known this strip of coast and delighted in it will miss the quality which is hardest to find along the most noisy of beautiful shores.

143

# Naples

Above us, winding over the mountains, is the old mule path which was for centuries the only land link between Castellamare and Sorrento—a path so beautiful that every loiterer round this coast should follow it in the spring, pushing his way at times through overgrown bushes and brambles alive with yellow and blue butter-flies ; at times breaking into little stony rock paths, up or down the ravines, or by streams black with tadpoles, tiny "sirens of the ditch," as Tasso calls them. Many a legend of brigandage once haunted this path, about which such delicious calm now reigns.

Within the ten miles of coast-line between the two towns, some seven or eight old Roman towns and fishing villages overlap one another, or hide almost unnoticed within the curves of the shore. The most important is the Roman town of Vico Equesne. In its ex-cathedral are some of the best paintings of Bonito, an eighteenth-century artist and native of Castellamare, whose now-neglected works are scattered all over Naples. Morelli, I believe, made an effort to rescue some of his works from oblivion. There are also some sulphur springs, fitted for modern use, and for nearly a mile the air is full of their faint fumes, pleasanter than the powerful odour of the tanneries outside Castellamare. Some of these springs lie so near the shore that they must surely have been under water before the sea retreated in 79. Now we skirt an unbroken succession of enchanting bays, and a long range of hills sloping down to the sea, the highest S. Angelo, which, thickly clad with chestnut trees, is midway towards Sorrento. Many deep curves do we follow inland ; yet we come out almost at the point we entered, distances being curiously deceptive along the whole coast. Passing over the bridge which traverses a wide ravine near Meta, the road runs inland along the side of hills where upwards of thirty terraces may be counted rising from far below in the green depths of the gorge to far overhead. At certain parts of the road little children run to meet us, waving flowers or orange boughs. Like wood-nymphs they run lightly through the white dust with their bare feet, laughing and clamouring for sous. Wearily as this eternal cry falls on the ear, at least it is a delight to see such sun-flushed and smiling faces. In Meta is the house of Gianbattista della Porta, the inventor of the Camera Obscura, and the founder of that fantastically named Academy in Naples, the *Oziosi*. The house was traced a short time past by Signor di Giacomo.

From Meta to the parish of the Trinita, where there is one of the best examples of Ippolito Borghese's work —the Resurrection—we pass through orange groves ; then comes the little town of S. Agnello, the land of Giacomo de Castro, many of whose works fill the neighbouring churches. As the danger limits of Vesuvius are distanced, S. Gennarius is forgotten and the more peaceful images of Madonna and Child are around us. We are on a road of Madonna's shrines and legends. They hide under the drooping trellis of leaves at the corners of sunny walls, or rise high against the houses under the creepers. Over one white-washed shrine the ripe oranges tremble under the trees. Over another, marking the turn into a mountain path, roses and wistaria have twined together a web of flowers; and there is yet another, near which the mustard plant glows like gold, while within it there is a tiny natural garden. To the stranger, already filled with the tender charm of this land, these continual and simple signs of religious feeling seem quite idealistic; but many are the romantic illusions in Italy which vanish as we delve beneath its lovely surface. The religion of the poor is but a debased Paganism without the spontaneous spirit of Pagan days. These shrines show the worship of not one Madonna, but of countless local deities, who often change in popularity as easily as the most trifling fashion, and an unanswered prayer will rouse a sentiment of revenge which is often expressed by either totally neglecting the Madonna's shrine or locking it up so that no offerings can reach her. It is the same unreasoning rage with which the Neapolitans insult the bronze statue of their patron saint by terming him "Yellow Face" when the liquefying of the blood is too slow. Unfortunately, the great Madonna-worship about Naples, so full of the natural poetry of the people, is often a means among the dishonest of acquiring money and confiscating the humble offerings of the poor, as in the case of the Madonna della Pignasecca. When one of these frauds was discovered, and all the gifts of the faithful were found to have been squandered in the hands of the Camorristi, a Frenchman asked a poor woman what was the use of money given for such a purpose. "Excellenza," she answered, "we give to the

CATHEDRAL OF AMALFI

Overlooking the busy piazza, the public fountain,
and the fruit market.

# Sorrento

Madonna, and the intention in our heart is a good one ; if others steal the money, what does it matter to us ? "

A gentle slope leads down to the sheltered table-land on which stands Sorrento, the little town without a history. Travellers pass through it, but know little or nothing of its past. For them it is the smiling town where oranges, lemons, and olives have ever flourished. Yet once it was barren of this later-day " Agrumi," [1] and not till the sixteenth century, perhaps, had the growth of oranges become sufficiently luxuriant to beautify the hillsides. Among the several sirens up and down this coast—at Panormus, at Naples, and at Capri, whence they passed to the rocks that bear their name— a few haunted Surrentum and its smiling and clear waters ; but they have left no legends, as their sisters did. If indeed S. Anthony once preached here, saints do not make history. Few are the landmarks of the past : nothing is old, and nothing has been written in stone. The perishable tufa of which the buildings are constructed crumbles like dust when touched with the finger of Time, and when Time might pass it over the waves of the sea wash them away as surely as they swept away the little house where Tasso was born, of which Lamartine wrote : " Quand l'horizon du matin était limpide, je voyais briller la maison blanche de Tasse, suspendue comme un nid de cygne au sommet d'une falaise de rocher jaune coupé à pic par les flots ! " Greeks and Romans have dwelt here, yet nothing of their vitality remains, save perhaps a tincture of old

[1] " Agrumi "—word comprising all oranges and lemons.

147

blood that may still course through the veins of this little-changing people, and may still speak in the proverbial beauty of the women, and in the curious insularity of the Sorrentian, which has in it a touch of the ancients' contempt for " barbarians " ; or save in the old foundations of some Roman basilica, on which the cottages of the poor have been long grafted. Only a few traditions, a few legends, haunt the little town which would otherwise seem without a yesterday.

> " Napoli bella, Sorrento civile,
> 'Chi venga ammalato a Sorrento si sana,"

wrote a native poet with less rhyme than reason ; but in his simple words are embodied its whole story from the days of the Romans down to our own times. It is one of the healthiest of spots, as the brown and richly tinted faces of the inhabitants bear witness ; the children's cheeks are as rosy as the coral beads about their necks, which here they need only wear as ornaments, and not as charms against the childish fevers which haunted the Roman children of long ago.

Some sixty years ago travellers who passed this way rarely lingered long. "Sorrento is not much of a place," said a well-known writer twenty years ago, and no doubt it was still less of a place in those earlier days. There was then but one hotel in Sorrento—the old Jesuit Convent, the Albergo Cocumella. In 1846 the Hôtel Syréné was opened. Now it is a little town of many hotels with lovely gardens—gardens which possess that strange character which is the result of a combination of English flower-beds, Italian fruit-trees, ornamental jars, and stone seats. The difference is wide between the natural *orto* of the Italian and the garden of the North in which every flower has been planted and trained with care. Here the growth of flowers is a wild thing that will not be tamed. Roses, violets, trails of hanging wistaria, bloom outside the garden walls, while within flourish the more-tended fruit-trees, the figs and pomegranates, peas and asparagus, pots of basil and sweet lemon : "A poverty of flower gardens and richness of pots," as Vernon Lee describes it. Till within quite recent years flowers have played but a small part in the lives of Neapolitan ladies. A very few have now sought to revive the old Roman culture of roses, purely for their pleasure—an advance in itself on the Roman spirit which delighted more in the reckless destruction of rose-leaves at festivals, or for their essences, than for aught else. I recall a Neapolitan lady who cultivates roses with real enthusiasm in her lovely garden of Naples, but is still looked upon as eccentric in her taste. Not, perhaps, since Pompeian days, when the *peristylium* of the private dwellings was filled with rare flowers only, and the fruit-trees of the *hortus* existed only on the painted panels closing them in, has there been a genuine garden about Naples. When, in the eighteenth century, the French parterre (a word used originally to describe carpets, and later flower-beds imitating them in colour and design) was interspersed with groups of trees and decorated with statues and ornaments, the fashion spread into the

South, where all French tastes were eagerly copied. But as a rule the Italian garden is still much as Martial sang to—where the vine gives its cool shade, the stream its clear water, and vegetables ripen in January unnipped by frost. Still, Italy more than any country gives the impression of being full of deserted gardens or enclosures, where flowers might once have been trained before the family grounds passed into peasants' fields. A broken statue, an empty stone vase with shell-like border, a rusty iron sun-dial fixed upon a wall, a low stone seat, warm in the neglected expanse where once shadows were trained—these are often found within a broken-down wall, or behind the twisted and fantastic scrolls of some old iron gate, " the gate that leads to nowhere."

I looked through the iron bars of such a gate near Sorrento. There lay the empty vase ; there stood the disused well in the midst of a perfect wilderness of vegetation. Lemons were glittering overhead, and a child was idly catching at the lizards' tails in the sun. Beyond rose a great rococo stone gate, pretentious and neglected. Nothing did it shut in, and nothing out. It is a curious fact that in all ruined towns, Fora, or walls, the gate resists time the longest.

To appreciate to the best advantage the curious position of Sorrento, between its narrow one-mile boundary of sea and mountain, turn into one of the long high-walled and serpentine roads that lead up into the hills. Every road going inland is the same. Between high green-stained walls over which orange-trees under

TERRACE OF THE CAPPUCINI HOTEI,
AMALFI

In full summer.

great tents of matting are visible, the rudely paved path leads up a gradual incline, silent and deserted. Like a serpent's tail it winds on past blue-tiled shrines and little dark rills of water, on and on, as if for ever. Then suddenly the wall ends, and the great view which follows us everywhere round the coast is again spread before us, and always does it seem new and wonderfully beautiful. Such a road leads from the market-place up to Piccolo S. Angelo. Another leads from the high road down towards the sea and to the gate of the Villa Crawford, which stands on a jutting ledge of rock over the water, and is hidden within a lovely garden. Great twisted trees of wistaria shade the drive, and through the leaves gleams a snow-white tennis-court with marble steps leading up to it as to some Greek Gymnasium.

A lovely climb leads to S. Agata ai due Golfi, and so on to the Deserta, the climax of all the Sorrentine views. In the Church of S. Agata is an altar of Florentine work, seventeenth century, in which are inlaid mother-o'-pearl, lapis-lazuli, and 'giallo rosso e verde antico.

Then, too, how many a little path leads into the heart of the orange country! The whole history of Sorrento is blended with the fruit. Think what a joy was denied to Virgil, who had but the rose, the immemorial vine, the sea-loving olive (which is said never to die), to sing to. There was the citron, it is true, which Pliny and the ancients seem to have confused with the orange; but the citron is in comparison a sad fruit—more of an antidote to poison than a delight, more *tristis* and *tardis* in its taste than sweet. When was the orange first freely cultivated round the coast? When did the perfumed "apple" first separate itself from all the other apples of strange medicinal qualities of the days of Theophrastus and the past? The first distinct mention comes in 1548, with the Arab invasion, when the sweet Portugali began to spread, and the Seville oranges reached even England, and were stuffed with cloves and other spices, to serve as a fashionable pomander. Yet De Falco, the curious old sixteenth-century guide (perhaps the first) to Naples, mentions the orange-trees " che *d' ogni tempo* spiriamo soavi odori per tante bianchi fiori " in the beautiful gardens of Chiaia. The Aragon kings are said to have shown a great taste in their time for these trees; and later, Don Pedro cultivated them with infinite care in the royal park. But the tree destined to change the whole scenery of this coast, and the very destiny of " ce peuple qui donnera la vie pour une orange," was still a quite artificial growth, only the luxurious pleasure of all the royal palaces of France and Italy. Now Sorrento is one of the orange centres of Italy. Millions of oranges pass on the boats to Santa Lucia, and the yearly blessing of the Agrumi is already merged in the centuries.

The most casual stranger who lingers at Sorrento must remark the great difference between the character of the Sorrentian and that of the Neapolitan. There is I know not what of primitiveness and naïveté about the Sorrentians. By this I mean, not that they are less practical or less interested, but that the traditional

THE STREET OF ATRANI

simplicity of a fisher population contrasts with the intellectual corruption of the over-sophisticated Neapolitan. This is a trait noticeable more or less in all the little fishing towns along the coast. The fisher-folks are robust and honest, fine types of healthy and hard-working men. They have, moreover, a strong individuality of their own, and a delicate, if intricate, sense of humour, all the more remarkable because humour plays so slight a part in the Italian character. The fact that this little population can intermarry almost entirely among themselves for so many generations, and produce such splendid types of physique, is a striking proof of their vitality. The deformities which fill the little towns of Italy produce here only a quaint stunted growth, still healthy and strong, human gargoyles with a dignity of their own, like the dwarfs of Velasquez. The women, too, may be said to be even stronger than the men. The work they do is often harder than that done by men—and that in spite of the enormous families they rear. Women, young and quite old, may be seen toiling along the road to Sorrento beneath burdens which even a Northern labourer would hesitate to fasten upon his back. They wear short petticoats, showing their bare legs, and feet bound with twisted rags to steady the ankles—a strange sight at first. They say "Buon giorno" light-heartedly as we pass them, and the sturdy simplicity of their lives is such that the problems which preoccupy us do not exist for them.

Perhaps the Sorrentians occasionally trade somewhat

on the stranger's belief in their native simplicity, and seem at times to realise that a little cunning among a sleepy people is refreshing to others. But the people of this *paese* are still far above the degradation of the dishonesty in Naples, where nothing is ever done except for money. An offer there to do anything " for love " must be distrusted—as when that Company who offered to build a home for the Little Sisters of the Poor (to all appearance so reasonably that it seemed, as they said, " per amore de Dio ") built it entirely without foundations. Unfortunately, there is a begging population here—large for so small and so prosperous a place. Rosy-cheeked and healthy children, and even well-dressed peasants, will beg audaciously. Beggars infest all this coast. The tourist evidently does not believe that it is better that " the lazy should die of hunger than be fed in idleness." The Greek and Egyptian spirit in which idleness was deserving of death would quite upset the modern travellers' delight in flinging coppers into the dust and watching their poorer brethren scramble for them.

Sorrento is, from its position, which turns towards the north, an ideal summer resort, although few foreigners seem to have discovered the fact. They haunt it during its rainy season, or early in April, when the snow is still lying unmelted upon the knees of Vesuvius. The rain falls very heavily in the spring, and the snow often lies thickly on the higher ranges of mountains. But on fine spring days no spot could present a brighter scene. The hotels are crowded;

the little streets are full of foreigners, buying tortoise-shell and useless silk scarves, or bargaining with absurd ignorance over the prices of inlaid wooden goods, so closely imitated by painted designs that strangers are often deceived, considering themselves very clever in getting for a few francs some object the only value of which is its imitation of the original. This work is best seen in the Art School of Sorrento, supervised by an old Garibaldian soldier and artist. There the work can be traced through its highly artistic unfinish, when it closely resembles a Pompeian fresco, to its polished and popular perfection, when all its artistic quality has been varnished away.

The time to see the place in its true glory is in the summer, and during the delightful Italian bathing season, which often lasts into October. There are vivid descriptions of summer life here in the novels of Mathilde Serao. Then the tourist season is over, and the villas round the coast and up in the hills are occupied by Neapolitan families. The uncertain climate, the torrents of rain, and the gusty winds, are gone ; days of exquisite warmth and starlit nights follow each other all through the summer months, and on into the autumn days, when the roads are strewn with fallen olives, the yellow dandelion springs from every rock, and the ruddy clusters of aloe blossoms are bright against the sky. Go into the market-place in the morning, and you will find a spectacle that cannot be surpassed for picturesque charm. Part of this piazza is built over the great gorge beginning in the hills and descending rapidly to the sea, and once a roaring torrent must have dashed down the ravine. The line of the old town wall of mediæval times which once followed it has now disappeared and has given place to a fine road. Crumbling ruins are incongruous in Sorrento, and the hand of man has not been idle in helping to remove them. On one side of the Piazza the bright plaster façade of a little rococo church and the pink and yellow houses glitter in the sun. A splendid sweep of hills forms the background of this picture. In colour these hills behind Sorrento run to the deepest blue, and in the early morning mists great wreaths of clouds hang about them delightfully, now hiding, now revealing some distant habitation or rugged mountain precipice ; or, again, some wild garden of olives and dim tufa rocks. On the other side the sea gleams through the steep defile of precipitous rock overgrown with the most lovely wilderness of creepers, which here run sheer down to the shore. All is light and movement in the market. Mules with shining brass ornaments, and harness which is literally made up of charms and prophylactics, are descending from the hills, down the mountain paths. Rich masses of autumn fruits and vegetables are piled on the pavement in the square. When the red water-melons of summer are over, comes the season for the green and black figs, together with strings of tomatoes, baskets of the sweet *fravole-uva*, with its double flavour of grape and strawberry, and the gorgeous scarlet *peperoni*. All is massed up together, side by side with the colour of the medlars and that of the shining

GARDEN IN THE VILLA PALUMBO,
RAVELLO

A mass of flowers in the spring season.

chestnuts. Eager groups of buyers and sellers are chattering over their merchandise. Oh, this eternal bargaining of the South! What a zest it gives to the daily routine of life! I saw a small boy, certainly not more than ten years of age, trying to sell some half-dozen coloured handkerchiefs to the girls about the place. Each girl seized one of the gaudy fichus of cotton, shook it out of its neat folds, tossed it from hand to hand among her companions with critical remarks, and finally offered him three of the six soldi he had asked. The poor little wretch could not come down in his price on his own responsibility, and after twenty minutes of useless haggling the dishevelled hand-kerchiefs were thrown back to him contemptuously. During the scene the girls were munching at enormous loaves of bread, which they held under one arm, tearing pieces off. At the height of the bargaining a big boy was busily devouring the loaf from behind the arm of one of the haggling girls. I felt quite sorry for the urchin, who looked both hungry and unspeakably weary of feminine society; but no doubt these are the early struggles that form the character of manhood.

Quarrels are rare here; but when they do occur the vociferation is endless, and the whole Piazza stands round and watches with interest. A veritable chorus of Aristophanes.

Perhaps one of the most picturesque sights from an artistic point of view is the wide, low fountain in the Via Tasso, which stands above three shining and dripping steps, which the naked-footed children, and the clattering sabots of the men and women, mount and descend countless times each day. Here the women wash and fill their great copper mezzini and terra-cotta bowls, and here the mules and donkeys slake their thirst. Let us hope that a few among the crowds of tourists who pass by pause before it and sometimes delight in its stained and many-tinted walls and beautiful proportions, even though the guide-books have passed it over. Two dolphins, with tails entwined, pour a continual jet of water into a marble basin encrusted with moss and lichens, a veritable fantasy of the Renaissance.

The intense languor of summer life in Sorrento is less felt perhaps by foreigners than by the Neapolitans themselves. We are saturated with the energy of a stiffer climate; but they are a people who have been for centuries hypnotised by the glittering sea. "We turn our backs to it when we wish to work," they say; but even that is difficult when every window, balcony, and loggia looks right over the water. During the long and lazy day the sea-bathing naturally occupies much time, both for the bathers themselves and for those who look on, or rather down, at the gay scene in the water beneath the rocks. Towards evening crowds of children swarm upon the beach, dashing in and out among the waves, and shouting with delight. On the warm nights, too, we bathed by moonlight in water full of phosphorescent flame. Through the dark could be seen the ruddy torches of the fishermen spearing eels, and away beyond all was the red lava pouring down the side of Vesuvius. Such scenes are unforgettable, especially for

CATHEDRAL OF RAVELLO

As seen from the terrace of the Villa Palumbo.

the Northern mind, leaving, as it were, an inextinguishable summer in the memory.

"The clear sea-waves are rushing about the coast of Sorrento,
Still do I hear in my dreaming their distant and elf-wild music,
Still see the white foam tossed far beneath at the feet of the city,
Filling the hollow of grottos, of cavernous stony recesses.
The perfume of sweet orange groves rolls down the height of the
    mountain,
Rolls down the rocks that the zephyrs float so lightly away from,
Thrust, as it were, from the woods far above too perfumed to
    hold them.
Here, when the sea-breath is cool and tempers the radiant sun-
    shine,
When we see far across the Bay, Naples, and near it Vesuvius,
We marvel then at the spirit that such a world has created,
A world eternal and wondrous, as wondrous as it is eternal." [1]

From no other point is there such an admirable *coup d'œil* of the Bay of Naples. It dominates the scene ; its long descending lines sweep gradually to the sea, and vanish insensibly into the clustering towns, which it seems to thrust almost into the blue water. No more fairy-like effect could be imagined than the glitter of distant myriads of white houses shining in the sunlight, massed thickly upon the shore, but more scattered as they ascend the first gentle slope of the mountain towards where the vines of the lacrymæ Christi grow out of their bed of ashes. The whole coast-line which lately we followed in the railway lies before us. Castellamare, Torre del Annunziata, Torre del Greco, Portici, and finally Naples itself, shine like

[1] Translation from the German of Kopisch.

a diadem of pearls round the azure sea. Over all the dreamy summit of Vesuvius blends its slow volume of smoke with the cloudland that rests upon it. On a clear summer night it is equally beautiful and more mysterious. The town lights of Naples twinkle across the bay, and seem but a stone's-throw off. Now and then a lurid gleam from the crater reminds us of the sleepless forces of the under-world. I never realised so well the magnificent description of Etna in the *Æneid*, in which the poet speaks of the mountain as "licking the stars" (*sidera lambit*), as when looking across this bay on such a summer's night. Here the starlight is superb, and the red tongue of reflected flame seems to touch the heavens. A summer's night at Sorrento is intoxicating in its charm of sight, of sound, and of scent. Perfect stillness is over all ; the low plashing of waves at the foot of the cliffs seems mystic and far away. The air is full of delicate perfume of flowers and the sweetness of inland country. Except for the moonlight dancing on the waves, we might fancy ourselves miles from the shores, for no breath of salt brine from the tideless sea is in the air. The breezes of these summer nights are gentle beyond words, and little effort is it to the imagination to feel the myth-making spirit of the past fill our belief with the living personalities of the winds. Was it in one of these rock-bound caverns beneath us that Æolus held his court and ruled the coming and going of the Notus and the Auster ? On a night like this Zephyrus alone is present, caressing us with his gentle breath. The waves at our feet are peopled with Nereids and Tritons, as the air is full of the voice of the living wind. The great pantheism of antiquity is spread out before us in the starry vault above ; and we think insensibly of the invocation to the great Huntress :

> " The risen stars and the fallen cling to her,
>     And the South-west wind and the West wind sing."

The stone pines murmur as the wind freshens, and Nature seems indeed to reveal the existence of Gods everywhere.

Far beneath us the dark waves are washing over those lava blocks of regular form which often we have looked down upon through the clear and sunlit water —the foundations of those vanished summer villas of the Romans, from which they too looked across the bay on many such a night.

# CHAPTER IX

## AMALFI

" Far beneath us lies as it were an abyss of destruction ;
Step out on yonder terrace, and in the vaporous distance
See low down on the shore round the curves of the bay before us,
Low on its edge by the sea, silhouetted magnificent columns.
Side by side they stand, like a primitive forest of sculpture,
Perfect, Doric, and still.   Round the roots only lizards are darting,
And over its vast aisles, now, only the ravens are flying."
<br>Von Platen.   (Translated from the German.)

ALL travellers have felt that there is sometimes a vague
familiarity about things and places never seen before,
which leaves us in doubt as to whether some delicate
thread of memory that once bound us to a past existence
has not been broken.   To each new spot we seem to
bring a new self or an old self that was forgotten.
Whether a place gains more for us through memory
or through the unknown would be hard to say ; but
many a traveller to the South of Italy will have felt
this dreamy familiarity following him round the Bay
of Naples to Sorrento.   Round the coast to Amalfi,
however, all is new and wild, remaining so even to
those who return again and again.   There is, as it

162

GARDEN OF THE PALAZZO RUFFOLO,
RAVELLO

were, a changeless strangeness in the majestic rocks
to which time has given the forms of ruined fortresses
of still invincible strength, or the primitive human
outline of monk or prophetess with outstretched hand
half escaping from the stone, like the imprisoned souls
of Rodin. A mere thread breaks the descent from
the heights to the sea, and along that thread of white
road horses and carriages race past with jingling of
bells and lashing of whips, while over the edge of
childishly protective wall we gaze down into the clear-
ness of the water where

"The wind on the warm sea dozes."

Half-way between Sorrento and Positano are seen
through the aloes and olive groves the Isles of the
Sirens. Tiny and wave-swept as they are, there they
lie unchanged, as far as we can tell, since the days of
antiquity, and the name of the "Fascinators of men"
has clung to the little archipelago of islets, the longest
of which measures only a quarter of a mile in length.
Why the name of the "Galli" is now used nobody
seems very sure; nor why beings so harmful as the
sirens should ever have had their image converted a
century or two ago into amulets. "Selonc la verité
les Sireines furent III. meretrix qui decevorent tous
les trespassares et les metrient en poureté," and only
the wily Ulysses escaped from their death song. Why
then did Dante write

"Io volse Ulisse del suo camino vago
    Al canto mio"?

163

# Naples

Positano, which lies midway between Sorrento and Amalfi, is quaint and delightful. The town itself is built below the high road, towards the shore, and with a picturesque piazza and cathedral. On one side of this piazza stands a little dark pharmacy, a veritable curiosity shop within, lined with eighteenth-century chairs, and decorated with shelf above shelf of those rare old pharmacy jars which collectors love, and which are every day becoming harder to find. Behind the counter stood some enormous blue and yellow pots with seventeenth-century dates on their fat sides, and we looked at them with covetous eyes. But not for lucre could these rare specimens be bought. They were heirlooms which their owner would not have parted with for any sum of money—a rare characteristic in this country. "You are not the first to covet these jars," said the chemist with pride. "In my father's time an Englishman came here and desired, like you, to possess one, the duplicate of this before you. He offered a thousand francs for it, which my father refused; but he gave the jar to the Englishman because he was his friend." The pharmacies of the sixteenth century were always decorated with porcelain jars, the older ones having a spout, and all bearing quaint inscriptions upon their sides. Quite useless though they are in our time, they have still a lingering utility in such out-of-the-way spots as this, just as in the modern chemist's shop the great globes of coloured glass still remind us of their primitive use of attracting from afar the attention of the passers-by.

TERRACE OF THE PALAZZO RUFFOLO,
RAVELLO

One of the most romantic ot gardens in Italy.

# Amalfi

Leaving Positano behind we find the scenery becoming grander and more impressive. If it be possible to enjoy keenly yet solemnly, the beauty of this coast can be so enjoyed. The voice heard round this echoing world of rock and sea is far more the rare voice of Nature, undrowned by the sounds of man, than can be heard among the orange groves that lie behind its heights. Not a shrine marks the path of man's creed, and the tiny terraces of laborious handiwork seem trifling and insignificant amid such gorges of stone. Hardly a goat nibbles at the pale cactus-leaves of Sicilian memories. There is a loneliness, a stillness, that harmonises not only with the beauty around but also with ourselves, and the thoughts that rise as naturally within us as the moonlight sparkles upon the sea, and for a moment at least, amid such beauty, the earth-bound soul is "competent to gain heights that it may not keep." Few are those places whose charm can speak twice to us with the same voice, however eagerly we would hear it again, yet each time we pass round this drive the same sense of strangeness, of separateness from the banality of travel meets us. For travel *is* banal in our day, and even the value of "impressionist" impressions of travellers is questionable. One writer at least expresses this opinion in his own *Sensations d'Italie* : ". . . Je ne crois aucunement à la valeur des observations de route. . . . Sensations d'histoire, sensations d'art, sensations de nature—quand vous avez laissé pendant des semaines les trois courants déborder, jouer à leur gré sur vous, il se produit dans votre être intime un phénomène qui

# Naples

explique pourquoi chaque voyage se termine sur un changement sécret de votre personne." Yet, if Nature speaks to each being with a different voice—if, in describing her, we "write ourselves down whether we will or not,"—then first impressions of travel must have some touch of freshness which, though of no lasting value, is *déjà quelque chose*.

Certainly there are some impressions true enough to be re-found each time a spot is revisited, and the same ones await us ever at Amalfi—the same conviction of its rare loveliness, and the same disgust for the degraded Amalfians who quarrel and beg and sleep away the days of divine sunshine in changeless squalor. It is difficult to believe that Amalfi was but a short time ago an active centre of the macaroni trade, so entirely has it now dwindled away. But we are, as it were, upon its classic ground, though macaroni in Italy is probably older than any one knows for a certainty—it may even have been included among the *pasta* of Roman days. It is curious how slowly this food grew into popularity, and what long and inexplicable lapses of time lie between its rare mention in the past, while the few authors who cite it in their works treat it always as more of a novelty of their time than as being familiar to them. Marlino Coccaja, one of the most famous of the early sixteenth-century macaronic poets, describes the dish as *rusticanum* and as if it was but little known, and Skippon, who travelled all over Italy in the seventeenth century and frequently commented upon the native food, makes no remark on this. We know that it was known in

# Amalfi

England in the time of Ben Jonson, though very super-ficially, since it was again introduced a century later, and then as a delicate dainty at Almack's, while the name of the *pasta* served as nickname to the absurd gallants who brought it over. But macaroni has persistently resisted taking root in England. Rowlandson, an intelligent traveller of the eighteenth century, was so struck with its excellence as a staple of nourishment that he urged its use in our navy—in vain! Macaroni may be said to have reached its present popularity early in the last century, and (to quote another old traveller) Whiteside, when he went to Ischia in the 'forties, says that he found there nothing but "beds and macaroni."

To return to Amalfi. When we have rounded the last jutting point and (if it be an early summer evening) approached it through air literally blazing with fireflies, the town rises before us, clinging to the rock much as a cluster of sea-anemones cling to the rocks beneath the water. Its structure is as fanciful as one of the weird conceptions of Victor Hugo embodied in his drawings. Beautiful is it as a vision—a vision to be remembered only, and not re-found ; for soon the fact is borne in on us that the real Amalfi is not what historic memories and sentiment and wayward imagina-tion had made it seem. What a writer said of it some fifty years ago is equally true of the present : "Amalfi is a dirty place ; in fact, an Augean stable." By a humorous playfulness of fate, the manufacture of soap is one of its especial trades. But it is one of the characteristics of small Italian towns that human dirt seems to add to instead of detracting from their charm. Into the beauty of the South all things fit, sad things and even dirt, though the dirt is not always that of the ground, which, as Warner says, keeps us pure. There are corners of Amalfi, up its one climbing street, where the neglect of ages has gathered together every imaginable tint of green, every mysterious shade of colours too soft for names ; and these dim spots are grateful to the eye dazzled with the expanse of sea and sky towards which all Amalfi turns. Here children who seem to have something really wild and primitive about them play and quarrel with dogs and cats, not more wild than themselves, all the long day ; or at the sight of a stranger they will spring away from their play and beseech for soldi. "Moio di fama," cries a little girl with rosy face. "Moio, moio di fama," echoes the fat child she holds in her arms. The begging on every side is quite terrible. To smile at a child—and how natural does that seem—without giving it a copper is an absolute waste of kindness.

"If I remain here much longer I shall beg for soldi myself," exclaimed an Englishman ; and he hurried away from Amalfi with real fear and disgust, reminding us of the story of the prelate sent to clean out one of the monasteries of the South, who was obliged to throw up his task and flee for fear of becoming himself as much lost morally as those around him. "Forgive them, your Holiness," he said. "It is in the air : I felt it myself."

Children usually appear to defy dirt more easily than

PULPIT OF SAN GIOVANNI DEL TORO,
RAVELLO

One of the two fine monuments of Byzantine work
to be found here.

# Amalfi

older people, or at least not to grow quite so revolting
under it ; but in Amalfi even the babies look old and
curiously unchildlike in their neglect.   I have seen them
plunged bodily, head downwards, into the fountain of
the Piazza, but apparently more to let them quench
their thirst than from any desire of cleanliness.   The
little girls wear their hair, often of a lovely golden
colour, twisted up into a tight roll behind the head, but
never do they look other than utterly and contentedly
squalid.   What a contrast is there between the bright
good looks of the Sorrento women and the almost total
lack of beauty among those of Amalfi !   All look alike
in their absence of freshness and in a somewhat degraded
type not pleasant to witness.   Perhaps the people of all
places that have sunk from a great past into such utter
insignificance strike us as degraded.   These people were
once as the children of a beneficent Nature who had
lavished upon them magnificent coast-lines and rich
naval possibilities, and when the sea in a single night
swept into its depths for ever those gifts from which
they may be said to have sprung, they also sank,
morally, into the deep.

It is a relief to turn towards the noble Cathedral,
that fantastic growth of every kind of architecture save
the Greek, enriched from so many ages of art down to the
sweeping coat of paint of our own day, which rises far
above the Piazza with indescribable beauty.   Here we
come across the first foreshadowings of the past days of
Paestum, and its devastation will be familiar long before
the ruined grandeur of its temples is before the eyes,

# Naples

for tradition as well as historic fact has grafted spoils
into the cathedrals of Amalfi and Salerno. Here, in
the cloisters of S. Andrea, are encased and hidden in
wretched wooden supports those crumbling columns
which once adorned its portico, fitting even into the
structure of Norman and Lombard days, for the
sculpture of the great past still keeps its secret of
perfect harmony.

Perhaps nothing is rarer than to see the riches of
past handiwork on the very spot for which it was
designed, and here, far above us in the Campanili,
"glittering like a dragon's tail," the purple of the
mountains now lies darkly against those Corinthian
pillars of a later-day Paestum which must long ago
have gleamed like the white stems of flowers in the
midst of the rose-gardens.

In the Piazza at the foot of the Cathedral's sixty
steps stands the fountain, the heart and pulse of the
little town. The basin is fine, but the centre decoration
of S. Andrea burdened with fish and artificial flowers is
almost uniquely ugly, a strange thing in a land where
lovely fountains abound as they have ever done from
the days when Boccaccio visited this coast and found it
"pieno di picciole città, di giardini, e di Fontane."
How clearly does the word convey to the mind's eye
a vision of marble and running water which combine
delightfully together with shining of wet sunshine and
plashing of playful music! No one can visit Italy
without being struck with this. Far back into times
of antiquity the cult for decorative springs existed,

OLD TOWER ON THE SHORE OF MAIORI

One of the many similar defensive constructions of
the middle ages against Saracen pirates.

and we know how the Renaissance, which quaffed so deeply from the wells of the past, delighted in their revival. But there is a kind of fountain produced in the South which is indicative of the natural artistic feeling of the people : a certain harmonious touch between the hand of the worker and Nature, which makes the polished cups and basins seem as if they had grown of themselves beneath the running streams of water. As if the people had understood that

> " . . . la source d'une eau saillante d'un rocher
> Est plus douce au passant pour sa soif estancher
> (Quand sans art elle coule en sa veine rustique)
> Que n'est une fontaine en marbre magnifique,
> Par contraincte sortant d'un grand tuyau doré
> Au milieu de la cour d'un palais honoré." [1]

Every village of the South is marked by a more elaborate fountain, which stands as the heart of the life and ways of the people, and round it a ceaseless stream of natives passes from morn till night. All the washing and all the drinking seems done here ; all that strange wild talk which is as mere gibberish to the stranger, so ceaseless is it and so careless of the hours that pass—all stirs round the marble heart of this empty shell of the past. We watch the burning dark faces bending over it, and the water splashing up and over them, and overflowing till it trickles far along over the stones to where a fruit-stall juts from a corner with a blaze of oranges and tomatoes. How many are the pictures that arrest the eye on every side ! Would that they could remain

[1] Ronsard.

and that too much gazing did not wither the freshness from these scenes. But travellers bring from other lands something of the *jettatura* in their eyes ; or is it only in their gold ?

In the dark shadows under the walls and up the Cathedral steps men and children lie sleeping, face downwards, with the flies buzzing over them ; and the little green lizards, or sometimes even their brown companions of poisonous reputation, creep out of the stones and bask beside them in the sun. Never do we see a woman sleeping. A jar upon the head, a child in the arm, a half-knitted sock on long curved needles between the fingers,—for them there seems no time for slumber. The air is full of that weird odour of back streets full of such infinite variety, and so strong that not even the breezes of the open sea or the sweet breath of orange blossom on the terraces above can sweep it away. At moments it reminds the most stoical of travellers that one torment in Dante's hell—a torment which, curiously enough, has been the least treated of in the ages that gloated over horrors—really *would* be beyond endurance.

The scene in Amalfi is ever idle, yet how restless ! Or is it that all idleness appears so, and only the sweat of man's brow gives the calm which spreads such a charm about a country ? No calm is there in Amalfi. The once-quiet mediæval cloisters of the Capucini, so familiar from the photographs " con monaco e senza," are now as noisy as the street beneath, where the unfortunate tourist can be seen, followed by a crowd of begging poor, all making loud personal remarks and laughing among themselves at him and at everything. The Amalfian's thought is his speech: he has no other. "Chi parla semina" is the only half of the old proverb that he seems to understand.

Yet what a spot must this once have been to withdraw to from the world, whose restlessness is spread far below, while here nought but the distant and low-toned echo of it reaches! Surely the cult for monastic life in the past expresses not only a devout sentiment but also a deeply-rooted passion for solitude—a belief that in it lay all the nirvana which disillusioned heart or incomplete existence could need. It is the very spot from which the following lines might have been written:—

> "Into the road I threw this heart of mine
> And far up on a mountain have I flown.
> There, for Love's story and its passionate sorrow,
> S. Francis took me, poor monk, for his own.
>
> "Tap, tap !—
>         Who's there ?—
>                 'Is there one here
> Who, down in the street let fall his heart ?'
> —Maiden, thou wilt not find such person here,
> With Mary's blessing and God's peace, depart.
>
> "Then chanting to herself the maiden sang,
> 'O Love, in a monk's life thou hast no rest !'
> And down the mountain-side she bore away
> The heart . . . hid 'neath the kerchief on her breast." [1]

Sometimes, in the tormenting street life, the one policeman who wanders about Amalfi—longing, no doubt, to lie down on the stones and sleep as so many

[1] Translated from the Neapolitan of *Il Monasterio*, di Giacomo.

of those about him are contentedly doing—takes pity on the exhausted strangers and beseeches the crowd to be more "discreto." I have seen him clasp his hands and simply implore the children to be reasonable; but in vain. This uselessly persuasive manner made me think him a being rather too kind for his business; but one day he showed a severer side. Our driver, who was waiting for us in the shadow of a wall, was tempted into deserting his vettura for a moment to go and help a comrade with a fallen horse. The policeman pounced upon his carriage, removed the dusty cushions inside, and bore them rapidly away to some spot from which they could only be reclaimed with a fine of two lire. But their owner looked more crestfallen than enraged. The Amalfians, like certain other races, take harshness and even blows stoically. "Per beata ch' ella non furon pesche." [1] Our driver shrugged his shoulders and muttered, "He is but a lazzaroni," and that is still a term which covers a multitude of sins.

No: in Amalfi there is no quiet, unless it be, perhaps, that, wandering on the shore or on the mountain paths far above the ruined arsenal where once the galleys of the Republic were kept, we may find a spot from which we ourselves unnoticed (oh, rare satisfaction!) can watch the fisherfolk spreading their dim red nets along the sands, and see the dark faces of the idlers leaning over the wall above, the one deep note in their world of Virgin's colours. These are the moments when, before its last narrow

---

[1] "Fortunately they are not peaches."—Old proverb.

# Amalfi

strip of beach, Amalfi lets us dream a few of all her prosperous dreams of the past, and we may picture the wide shore reaching from here far on to Maiori, its noble forts, its sheltering arsenal, its array of ships, many-oared, upon the beautiful horizon, where now not a single sail whitens the blue. For a moment we may catch the spirit of the middle ages, as we look across the bay to where Salerno may be imagined as preparing assault upon her fiery enemy. Yet all seems now but a legend, not of the earth but of the quiet sea : while something in the overhanging and cling- ing houses, the frowning rocks above and the calm but eager sea below, still murmurs of the fate which along these coasts of Italy has planted building above building as surely as the centuries have built their strata one above the other. A stony wound in the mountain's side, tragedy of quite recent date, seems even now to await fresh terraces and another smiling dwelling to reflect the sunshine on its windows and walls, since the homestead that lies beneath has hidden its face for ever.

The travelling spirit in the South is one of continual movement, and there are but few spots where lingering is habitual. Even while driving to Amalfi our vetturino was eager to discover the exact moment at which we intended "moving on" next day. The spirit of repose has been destroyed by the travellers themselves, and their determination to see all in a short time has so penetrated this sympathetic people that they never cease to remind us of the fact. Perhaps the reason of this restless spirit lies not only in the superficial character

175

of modern travel, but also in the formation of these fishing towns backed by rocks and bounded by a hot and shadeless road, of which, with the best intention in the world, one gets somewhat sick.

As this fine white road passes through Amalfi it naturally bears the name of the hypothetical Flavio Gioja, round whose individuality so much contradictory evidence has collected. In no record of his time or afterwards can his name be traced, though the two words forming it are undoubtedly connected with the mariner's compass. The Amalfians, borrowing the loadstone from the Arabs, adapted and spread its use upon the royal fleet of the Anjous, adorning it with the royal badge. This badge was used to mark the north on the compass, and consisted of a golden lily, a " bright jewel," the very meaning of the words " Flavio Gioja." But the history of the compass is legendary. All we know is that its use spread over Europe from Amalfi.

This, however, does not prevent the descendants of Flavio Gioja from existing. We know that they received the bounty of the king a century ago, and some natives assert that the family still lives in a village near.

But enough of Amalfi. From the lovely hills above where Ravello lies hidden, " le vent qui vient à travers la montagne " is calling us with as sweet a breath as at Sorrento, the breath of spring and its flowers. So, with luggage-laden carriage and cracking of whip, with a procession of filthy children flying after us through

## VIETRI

The Marina is peculiarly interesting. The overhanging rocks are incrusted with masses of maidenhair fern.

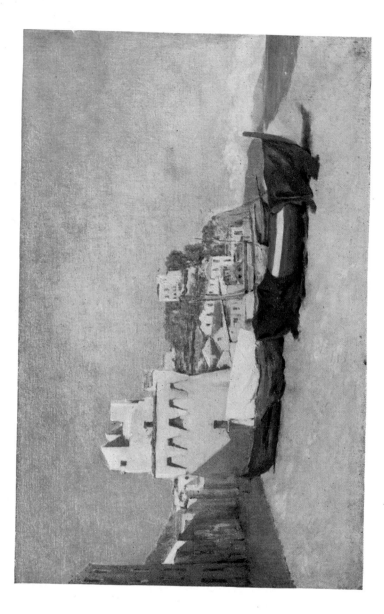

clouds of dust, we pass the shrine of the Stella Maris "che guide il marinaio con la sua stella," and, rattling through Atrani, the twin shadow of Amalfi, we turn to the left, where the way lies wide and smooth through the ravine of the Dragone, or Dragon's Tail, as it might be called, so brightly does it glitter with emerald scales. Masses of maidenhair on dripping rocks, fig-leaves thrust from the very stones, pink orchids and foxgloves, and a wilderness of common flowers, are above, while beneath hide the sheltered orange groves and the fast-disappearing flat-roofed houses of the peasants. An old sibyl crouching beside the roadside rises suddenly at the sight of a carriage, and with harsh and terrible voice shrieks a question into the silent gorge ; and a lovely echo murmurs back from another world.

At every turn of the road the air grows purer and the hills become more deeply green. High up across the ravine is perched the old town of Scala, which is said to have once possessed 130 churches, such a plethora of piety alone accounting for its extinction. It is curious how invariably these mountain towns kept their ecclesiastical independence although forming part of some greater centre, just as Scala and Ravello formed parts of the inland boundaries of Amalfi and made its greatness as did the sea-coast towns along its shores. The brief history of these mountain settlements is full of fascination, so totally different is it from the old-world history of Italy, the days when the Greeks chose lovely plains instead of heights on which to erect their cities. But in the middle ages, when piracy from the

Saracens had become a powerful factor, difficulty of access was the Italian's idea of safety—impregnable positions which made even small feudal holdings of great resisting power. Little wonder is it that these once powerful but too isolated fortresses soon passed into decay, when the great families who "made" the place, the gentlemen merchants of that time, gradually deserted their lonely castles, the pivots of endless quarrels.

As we approach Ravello we see but a little village with a ruined tower and a Cathedral despoiled of almost all its old-time beauty. Ravello may be termed the eagle's nest of the peninsula. I know of no place where the sentiment of lofty seclusion and repose is so enduring. After the jostle, heat, and dust of the routes by the shore, here we enter an atmosphere that is at once bracing and full of rest. The glorious gulf of Salerno lies below, and just above us a cloudland rests upon the hills ; and how distinctive and delicate is the charm of those hills! High as we are already, ravines slope higher still, here and there crested by some crumbling ruin or by a straggling mountain village on the white walls of which the sun glitters from time to time as the clouds part before its face. The bold gorges are deliciously clothed in verdure, and here the severity of the mountain forms has every outline softened by lovely vegetation. Steep descents to the sea lie on either side, one leading to Amalfi and the other to Minori. Among the vineyards of Ravello crumbling walls and Byzantine relics attest the past of

this beautiful place, and the breeze seems to murmur
with a strange sadness—

"Non sono io quel ch' un tempo fui."

The piazza, with its superb view, is bounded on one
side by a wide amphitheatrical stone seat, and opposite
to it rises the white-washed Cathedral, behind whose
green doors are hidden the masterpieces of Barisanus,
said to be unequalled save by the gates of the Baptistery
in Florence. Whatever were the vanished glories of
this Duomo, seldom is it that so supreme a work of art
as yet remains within can be found in so romantic a
position. We are accustomed to view masterpieces of
every kind in the stifling atmosphere of towns and in
the midst of the restless hum of men ; but this is one
of the rare instances to the contrary. Here a priceless
jewel of art is enthroned in a far-away setting of
natural beauty which adds an infinite charm. The
cutting of the jewel is worthy of its setting, and art
does not yield to nature in perfection. The severe
lines of the Byzantine structure are as gorgeous with
glittering mosaic as are the hills around with the mosaic
of nature.

The graceful columns supporting the famous pulpit
rest upon the backs of weird stunted lions, after the
fashion of the times. A dim green mould, time's
colouring, darkens them beneath. Above is an eagle
spellbound in the stone, as by a lingering touch of
Eastern conventionalism. As I gaze up at it the door
of the Church is open ; the lovely purple haze of the

hills glimmers outside, and air sweet with fragrance of flowers is wafted around this divine monument. The stone figures seem to brood, half-conscious of life, and the wings of the eagle appear to flutter as if it would fly far from its nest.

In the little church of del Toro stands another of these fine pulpits, rivalling it closely in beauty ; at the foot of its delicate columns tiny lions are crawling.

Wise are those who defy the gospel of the drivers and the guidebooks, and linger at Ravello. The air is life-giving. We are far above the warm languor of the shore which tempts to such drowsy enjoyment of life. There is an energy in the breezes which sweep around this spot, calling doubly to those who are themselves energetic and delight in action of mind and body, as well as in contemplative enjoyment of beauty.

THE BASILICA OF PAESTUM

On a May morning.

# CHAPTER X

PAESTUM

SOME day, perhaps, the lovely shore that lies between Amalfi and Salerno may become more popular as a winter resort, for its climate is soft and warm ; but at present it is still only a ground to be driven over, and even that often under difficulties, the horses at Amalfi being miserably bad and the drivers themselves little better. Its day has not yet dawned, and the beautiful Hotel del Torre still remains closed upon its majestic elevation. What a position for a dwelling! And beneath the rock upon which it stands there is a long stretch of beach—"real sand," as children say,—the blue water lapping it noiselessly. Jutting out to sea is one of the many towers of the South ; but the tower of Maiori is almost ruined, a dark and romantic silhouette on the sun-tipped rock from which it rises. The waves break softly round it, and one might almost imagine this one of the last spots on which the mermaids lingered, as they are said to have lingered in the belief of the Neapolitans, far on into the middle ages.

# Naples

Maiori is not so poor as Amalfi, and the people are not so incurably idle. The macaroni trade, which was once almost entirely Amalfian, seems to have drifted hither in a small measure. Instead of having rows of fishing-boats and nets, the shore is often seen completely spread over with sheets of the fine "spaghetti," too fragile to bear hanging out to dry. It looks as though the gray sands had turned to deeper gold in the hot sun.

After Maiori is passed the road winds up the mountain, curving ever in and out till another tower, the great tower of Cetara, comes in sight. This stands over a little fishing town, poor, but too primitive to know the misery of larger towns. Its inhabitants are still unspoiled by travellers, and are as industrious as the failing fishing trade allows. It is to artists that this place is dear,—who have for ages painted enthusiastically its humble beach and eccentric tower,—and among the oldest paintings of the south by foreign painters are found pictures of Cetara. It is a curious fact that places remind one of pictures far more often than pictures remind one of places. "Nature," as Whistler quaintly said, "is creeping up." The whole scene is typical of the days of Claude Lorraine, the days when Nature was painted from the purely fantastic rather than from the realistic point of view. For there is something wildly imaginative in the whole construction of this densely-crowded shore loaded with wave-washed boats, with complicated houses piled against the rocks, and

TEMPLE OF POSEIDON, PAESTUM

Best preserved of the three temples which adorn
the plain.

watched over by the magnificent tower whose edges catch the gleam of the sun when all else has sunk into shadow.

Like a mirage is the view of Salerno as it lies low upon the water's edge all purple and blended by distance. But, like a mirage, it fades away as we approach it, and nothing can be more wretched and colourless than the town itself. It is dreary to a degree, and whatever interest it has is the reflected charm of its background, the mountains of Salvator Rosa's muse, and of the wondrous temples of Paestum. The old story of its greatness seems to have no affinity with this straggling home of drowsy people, who for centuries looked across their bay at the grand Doric ruins sinking into their bed of wind-driven rubbish and earth without producing poet or artist to rescue them, or any attention of the learned. For ages the Salernian sailors and fisherfolk used them as their landmark,—the last use that great Poseidon bequeathed to his deserted dwellings. To the casual visitor, at least, the inhabitants seem poverty-stricken and diseased, while the walk along the sea and the pretty open garden of shady trees is crowded with perfectly idle men and women. It is much the same in the narrow back streets—those terrible streets where the air is filled with the nauseating smell of rotting vegetables, which the Neapolitans have, apparently from time immemorial, loved to tread into pulp under their feet.

Even the visit to the Cathedral is more of a

necessary evil than a delight, since it adds to the hours which one fails not to count in Salerno. This home of wonderfully preserved glass mosaic, so delicate that its preservation is one of the mysteries of time, has lost all its old harmony with its environment. If we are glad to see it, we are gladder still to leave it. Fortunately, the delight of the South of Italy lies greatly in the absence of museums and church interiors, and in the vast quantity of sun-pierced ruins open to the sky, which can be enjoyed without shutting out the freshness of nature. If museums are as tombs for the precious objects they enclose, the ruins of this country are alive with a deathless poetry.

Without having ever fallen into complete decline, Salerno has little of modern interest about it. Even its grand old tradition of medicine died out in the last century, when Villari, an ancestor of the great historian, lived here during the turbulent days of Ferdinand, and gained, in his way, a wide reputation. In the days when the South was cementing the unity of Italy Salerno woke up a little; but the history of Italy's great movement was the movement of its big towns only, contrasting curiously with the inertia of centuries in which the smaller centres slept on, only waking up, after all was over, to grapple with the question of emigration—a questionable improvement. Yet though it now belongs to the history of nearly half a century ago, the memorable night on which Garibaldi made his triumphant entry into the towns between bands of wild music and flaring torch-bearers must still be clear in the memory of the elders who saw the splendid countenance said to have borne such a striking resemblance to the busts of Euripides in the Vatican.

A curious old photographer lives in Salerno. He claims to have the secret of combining groups of the same person upon a light instead of upon a dark background. His work has received notice in England. His walls are covered with examples of stunted peasant types hideously multiplied to three. All the newly married and affianced couples visit him, the young girls arriving in their simple kerchiefs, and submitting, awestruck and blushing with pride, while he winds yards of pearl necklace about their necks, pearls as big and as hollow as soap-bubbles.

He kindly helped me to develop some films in his tiny dark room, but they were all fogged, for I discovered that he had left the door ajar, allowing the light to come through. I pointed this out to him, but his answer quite disarmed me : "I left it open, Signora," he said, "per delicatezza."

It would be difficult to forget the drive from Salerno to Cava on a warm evening early in June, or the fairy-like illumination of countless lucciole through which the way lies. Thousands upon thousands of white lights dance and throb around, till one is caught, as it were, in a quivering and glittering veil floating from the slopes above far down into the valley beneath. Their fire is full of the blending of the Spring with the Summer, the ripening of the barley and the corn.

# Naples

The Italian peasants believe that "the fireflies dancing above the ripening wheat are so many tiny living lamps of the sanctuary lit in honour of its future consecration, and thus offering their anticipatory service of adoration."

Strange indeed is it that this lovely "companion of the dew" should have escaped the poetic immortalising of the classic poets. The cicada was not beneath the notice of Anacreon, and the firefly, identical in so many ways with the glowworm, was undoubtedly known to Greeks and Romans of the classic age. This reserve towards one of the most striking features of a country points, perhaps, to some early mystic superstition in connection with the firefly, some conception of witch-craft which held them silent—not anything so terrifying as the belief of the Malays that the blood of murdered men turns into fireflies; yet they may have regarded the luminous insect as a distinct signal of hidden truths of the great book of Nature, from every closed page of which the "strage" of the past gathered their craft. In Leland's "Aradia" is given an old conjuration to Meal, from which I have made a rough translation of the beautiful Italian original :—

> "Whenever, O corn, thou wert pale and green
> Within folded ears, the fireflies came
> And cast o'er the fields their moonlight flame
> That thy growth in the dark might better be seen
> And perfection reached that the night might lose.
> So also, fireflies, you too belong
> To the witches' cantation, the Fairies' song,
> You belong to the great Sun, every one knows."

BASILICA OF PAESTUM

As seen on a May morning.

# Paestum

We have noted the silence of classic writers on this subject. What is no less striking in its way is the trivial part that this exquisite creature plays in the poetry of modern days. It is as though Dante's comparison between its wandering light and the circling fire of lost souls had lent a traditional gloom to its use in poetry. It is true that among the vast quantity of poetry written in the early part of the nineteenth century there are many allusions to the glowworm, and a few to the firefly, but they belong more to writers of a secondary order and of a sentimental school. Mrs. Opie's "Gem of the lone and silent vale," Mrs. Hemans' lines, Owen Meredith's comparison between the fireflies and "swarms of loving fancies, through some rich and pensive mind"—these are more fanciful than inspired. They belong, too, to poetry awakened by other countries, and not by the phenomena as blending into the peculiar beauty of Italian landscape. Even Browning, who so loved every aspect of Italy, hardly remembers more than that in his boyhood he

> "Plucked the fireflies from the roof above
> Bright creeping through the moss they love."

After a final steep climb, we reach Cava itself, which seems nothing but a winding street, so heavily arcaded that light and air are pretty well shut out, and so narrow and overcrowded that carriages and oxen, religious processions, weddings, and troops of idlers, become inextricably entangled. It lies in the midst of hotels where travellers sleep a night and pass a day, driving about through clouds of the thickest dust that the South is capable of producing. The life of the private villas is, of course, pleasanter ; for gardens are an absolute necessity to enjoyment during any stay in Cava. But if the town is far from attractive, the country around is unspoiled. It is a strange tameless landscape, where trees grow gnarled and dark, and long shadows lie in the valleys, and pyramidical mountains slope away and above, one beyond the other, crowned with cross or monastery or sculptured rock. Wild it is, and a name so coloured with romance and legend as is that of Salvator Rosa fits naturally into it. But did he ever paint here? Who can tell. Did he ever draw his whole inspiration for any one of his few works which remain to us from a single view of nature ? It was the fashion of his time to delight in mosaicing together a hundred foreign spots and fitting them into one, rather with the individuality of the painter's taste than with any strict slavery to Nature. All we know is that his youth belonged to Naples, and that the earliest and therefore strongest impressions of his strange mind belonged to the country round, though the greater part of his work itself belonged to Rome. But sometimes legends take as strong a hold in association as do dry facts, and the name of this one great Neapolitan painter is in the very air of the mountains as it blows down to us.

From Cava the railway goes directly to Paestum, passing through belts of green fields with great patches

## ON THE ROAD TO FORIO
Quaint wayside shrine overshadowed by oleander trees.

of golden flower, and in the background pale low-lying hills. It is one of the most vivid impressions that the South can give us—this first view of Paestum and its three temples, its ruined trinity of vanished power, all so old that Augustus visited them, even as we do in our day, as venerable antiquities whose birth was lost in the centuries.

A little country road bordered on one side with a hedge, on the other by rose-tinted walls over which a single pine throws a shadow and a group of laughing girls' faces look down upon the passers-by, leads from the station to the broad road and the meadows where the ruins rise into sight. It is a day in May, one of the first mild days when the sun has distilled into the air all the sweet warmness of the flowers. It is the season that poets love, and the artist finds too illusive for his art, though one at least, Constable, the lover of fresh greens, made it his own. On such a day the very blind would rejoice here, for sight is but one of the senses which Nature has satisfied. The luxury of the Spring vegetation round Paestum is beyond all words, seeming to laugh to scorn the legends of malaria and desolation. Even the asphodel, "bloodless blossom of death," which blooms as Spring dies, and is scattered around the ruins, seems with its pale flower to smile in the delicious warmth. The quiet of the spot is broken only by the cawing of the rooks, the low buzz of insects.

But the large and scented violets of which Shelley

speaks seem to have disappeared; and the roses of the Latin poets—where are they? We ask the question from sheer habit, since every writer on Paestum of our time asks the same. The twice-blooming flower—often thrice-blooming—whose euphonious name has fitted so perfectly into the poetry of every age and land, and has been more sung to than any other, deserted the gardens of Paestum—who can tell when? Roses are the flowers of silence, and mystery and silence are around the whole story of this Hellenic city.

Yet if any enterprising person undertook to plant the sweet strong rose de quatre saison here, I fancy they would grow as thickly as ever.

"Ah," said the station-master of Paestum, a quaint character, "what a wretched country this is! Did you ever see such a lazy people? They are ignorant, and they despise all agricultural knowledge. I am a Tuscan, and come from Perugia. If my country people had this land, they would make a veritable garden of Eden out of it."

"Well," said I, "what is that convent on the brow of the hill?"

"Don't ask me," he answered. "I know nothing about places of that sort. I call all that sort of thing a shame (*vergogna*). I am a pagan!"

It seemed that the poor man had lived here some fifteen years, a constant prey to malaria, which had evidently undermined his health not more completely than the relics of pagan days had poisoned his views of the religious condition of the country.

# Paestum

We skirted the luxuriant fields, all golden and purple with blossom, and paused to gaze up at the ruddy columns of the temple of Neptune. It is the very spot where the Greeks paused long ago, for here was the agora of the city. To the left rise the sea-gray ruins of the "Basilica." What words can justly describe them? There are moments when the poetry of beauty becomes, as it were, an atmosphere, and envelops us with an exquisite breath as we look at beautiful things; and here not only is it the sentiment of the past and of vanished lives, but also the tender poetry of Nature, that seems to gather into her arms this faded glory of man's handiwork as her especial child. There are temples more massive and more ancient in other lands which have fallen with the centuries into the semblance of tombs open to the sky, but with a gentler touch Nature has transformed the ruins of the Greeks into wild and lovely gardens. She has thrown her veil of greenery over the creviced stones, and high against the capitals of enduring travertine the sun-warmed purple flowers blossom and die with every year. Into the empty shell birds have poured their song, and the winds murmur through it like the waves of the sea.

The travertine of which the temples are composed is said to have been drawn from the neighbouring rivers, the waters of which were alternately sweet, or bitter and infected, according to the strength of its various sources.

Forgetting for a while that important business for

# Naples

which hundreds of tourists yearly visit the temples,—
namely, to eat their lunch in the shade of the austere
columns,—let us wander through the bracken to the
steps of the Basilica. This seems to me by far the
most impressive of the three ruins. There is something sublimely primitive in its vast wilderness of
massive Doric pillars, whose solidity and simplicity of
construction is softened by settled harmony of proportion, like the full chords of some mighty symphony
interpreted by the touch of a subtle musician. Add to
this the gentle hand of time that has filled the chinks
and crannies of stone with flowering blossoms and
many a patch of wild grass, carpeting the aisles with a
starry mosaic of Spring, and some conception may be
had of this wonderful wreck of time, where art and
nature have lavished their tenderest touches.

No other temple is said to present, as in this unique
façade, an unequal number of supports with the result
that a column marks the very centre of the entrance.
Little is known of the temple's history; and whether
its two aisles marked the double worship of Demeter
and her daughter or not, is still a matter of conjecture
gathered from the statuettes of the goddesses found
scattered around.

Of Poseidonia itself, almost all that is known of its
history is gathered from that one book of knowledge
which the city bequeathed to the archæologist, the
reading of its coins. It is they that tell us beyond all
doubt of its greatness and power, and of how on until
after the Social War it remained the only exception to

the stern law which forbade all local coinage in Italy other than that of Rome. Pieces of copper money bearing the effigies of Augustus and Tiberius, with the inscription of the authorisation which permitted their fabrication, are a condensed history in themselves.

Nevertheless, in spite of its early greatness, Poseidonia is said to have been the first of the chain of Hellenic colonies round the coast to succumb to Barbarians. Though the city regained its freedom for a second time, it was but for a brief period, a faint afterglow of the glory already set. With the progress of Christianity we hear more of Paestum, until it was finally and totally deserted. But never, surely, has a desertion so complete overtaken a spot of such poetic beauty on the very border of civilisation.

Though the Basilica has ever seemed to me the most grandiose of the three ruins of Paestum, the temple of Poseidonia is, of course, more perfectly preserved, and has always attracted a greater share of admiration. Its colour is of a rich golden tone, in striking contrast to the delicate gray of the adjacent Basilica. The ruddy tint disclosed by the fallen stucco is very like that of the temples in Sicily. One cannot help wondering as to what must have been the original effect of these three buildings when coloured, as they once were, by the architects of antiquity. Does the exquisite sense of form to which these remains testify imply a corresponding perfection in the sense of colour on the part of their builders? One would say from an inspection of the mural decorations of Pompeii that there, at least, colour played no distinctly subtle part, although always bright and pleasing. It might truly be said that Pompeian decorations belong to a decadent age ; but at the same time, if we can judge from the bronzes of Pompeii and Herculaneum, the feeling for form was still acute in that day, proving that the senses of form and colour were very unequally developed.

Perhaps the most important light that has been thrown upon this interesting question was the discovery in Asia Minor of the sarcophagus supposed to have been the tomb of Alexander the Great, which is now in the Museum of Constantinople. It is one of the rare examples in which both colour and form have come down to us uninjured and blending perfectly. Coloured sculpture has only of late years awakened interest among artists. The late Léon Gérome was one of the few searchers after this lost aspect of Greek art in antiquity, as the beautifully tinted statues produced towards the close of his life attest. The discovery of the masterpiece at Constantinople—a discovery made by a great friend of his—he regarded as of the first importance in the history of modern art ; and during the later years of his life we have heard him express with enthusiasm his admiration for the powers of the bygone masters who could " sculpt pictures and paint statues." If the effects of the painted sarcophagus is capable of producing such a profound impression, there seems to be no reason why the full-blown Greek temples, radiant in colours of the rainbow, should have been less delightful to the eye. And surely the prejudice

## THE TORRIONE, FORIO, ISCHIA

An interesting mediæval structure restored as a modern
dwelling by the Neapolitan sculptor, Giovanni Maltese.

against this blending of two arts is more the result of convention than anything more profound.

Well, the moment has come when, as mere hungry mortals, we seek a shady corner in which to break our fast. Let us eat with the goats nibbling at the food and the dreamy lizards watching us with their bright eyes. A young kid thrusts a too eager nose into the basket, but a child's voice calls it away by the laughing name of Bacchante, and it bounds off over the grassy wilderness into the burning sunshine. Little by little the place grows still. . . . A narrow file of figures laden with now empty baskets has vanished in the direction of the station ; but we linger on far into the glowing afternoon, resting amid the waving corn, and watching the ravens soar above their nests, black against the violet hills. No human being is in sight, save in the direction of the guardian's cottage, where the eternal business of Italian peasant life, the washing and hanging out of multi-coloured garments, is in full swing. What a part this lésivage plays in Italy ! Clothes are washed to rags while the body itself is looked upon as dirt-proof.

Even that tiny centre of life will disappear as the summer advances. The guard's house will be closed. The air, so deliciously sweet to-day, will become laden with poison, and the peasants for miles around will retreat with their pale-faced children towards the mountains. The poor station-master, that strange pagan character, will stoically fight his malarious foe with fever-stricken limbs. Even among the sturdy

# Naples

Buffalo tribes there will be some who succumb to the deadly ill.

We drove back to Salerno as the day fell and the rising breeze began to murmur through the corn. Flat and smooth winds the road between low-lying fields, across which the dim temples only fade by degrees from sight. They still mark for the ordinary tourist the boundary between the known and the unexplored land. Beyond them lies that wonderful country of the middle ages, Apulia and Lucania, where the modern conveniences of travel penetrate but slowly. " Les ruines de l'antique Poseidonia sont comme les Colonnes d'Hercule que l'on ne dépasse pas dans la direction du midi," says Lenormant. Strange indeed is that country wasted with malarious soil, where even that great God of Chance, the Lottery, hardly ever smiles. Among all the countries that play, Apulia is said to come off the worst.

Now and then we pass herds of buffaloes with fantastic horns, for we are on the classic ground of the tribe in Italy. Here they are said to have been first introduced from Sicily by the Norman kings, spreading gradually in vast numbers over parts of Calabria and the Roman Campania, haunting the marshy malarious lands, where they can stand knee-deep in the water. Themselves never completely tamable, wherever their tribe is seen there is something wild and solitary in the landscape ; and only as the ground becomes drained and reclaimed do they slowly yield place to their more homely kindred, the oxen.

We watched them wade in and out of the marshy

ditches, standing at times so stilly amid the straw-tinted growth about them that they seem to be listening to the "dreary melody of bedded reeds," to the sighing of the breeze through the stalks that Pan would not suffer to remain idle.

To all who are interested in the progress of Italy, the sight of the malarious parts of the country awakes an absorbing problem. The most striking feature of Southern Italy, from the agricultural point of view, is the vast extent of marsh land, covering a fifth of the territory, and almost wholly resisting cultivation. The Pontine marshes and the Maremma are the first witnesses of the deep misery which separates the north from the south ; but their extent is insignificant in comparison with the immense stretches of waste land which are comprised in Campania, Calabria, and Apulia. The ill is at the root of much of the stagnation of the south, and the true spirit of agriculture, the healthy struggle with ground and climate, seems curiously dormant among the landed proprietors. In Tuscany the owners live on their lands and personally supervise affairs ; but round Naples the great private farms and pasturage are neglected to an inconceivable degree. This aristocratic neglect has penetrated to the smaller tenants, who now often emigrate in large numbers for no other reason than that their untended land no longer produces sufficient to pay the usurer.

For forty miles the road winds from Paestum to Salerno, through a country where habits and costumes and manner of life are distinctly of past centuries. As

# Naples

we drive along under the branches of trees shimmering in the pale dust like some idyllic dream of Corot's, the poetic illusion is deepened by the traces of old times which meet us on the way. The contadini trudging along the roadside are dressed in the charming native costume which figures in the old paintings and prints of Italy—heirlooms which they are still proud to wear. These costumes of the past are quite different from those of Rome and the north. Every little village about Naples has, or lately had, its own distinctly native costume, which in a few spots is still seen in all its primitive gorgeousness. Not far from Naples itself there is a most interesting and curious bit of country, where on fête days the women wear, not extra jewelry, but an additional number of aprons, every apron adding to their respectability. The aprons are as often as not mere kerchiefs, but always of the richest silk and embroidery. It was not so very long ago—in Dickens's time, was it not?—that quite as unreasonable a fashion flourished in England, when many waistcoats were worn one above another.

As we drive along, an old postchaise rattles past with the arms of a vanished crown painted and faded on the door. But the most wonderful sight of all comes with the setting sun, when great gangs of young women labourers, singing uproariously and waving leafy branches, drove by in waggon-loads of thirty or more. Here, as in parts of Greece to-day, all the field labour is still done by women, and it would be difficult to find ruder types of health than among these gangs.

IN THE VILLA MARESCA

Near Casamicciola, Ischia, showing antique oil or
wine jars of unusual size.

# Paestum

The shrill voices follow us for miles, singing monotònous songs. There seem to be no distinctive native canzoni about Paestum, and it is noticeable that round the two gulfs, as Naples or Salerno is distanced, the popular melodies of the people grow scarcer. It is town rather than country life that produces the Neapolitan music and verse, and the more primitive countries are comparatively voiceless. "Quanno se canto non se pensa male" is somewhat contradictory round this coast.

If we leave Paestum without seeing a single rose, we shall find them on this long road leading into Salerno. There is a garden-wall that stretches along beside it for what seems over a mile, and over every inch of it the gay pink roses de quatre saisons are hanging. As if the shadows of the magnificent stone pines within were too heavy a vault for their delicate beauty, they escape over the wall into the bright sunshine and are a delight to the passer by.

> "The garden has spread
> All its heart to the rose ;
> And its breath—how it blows,
> With what perfumes fed :
> Is it better to gather
> The roses ?—no, rather ;
> Gaze, gladly, instead ! "[1]

[1] From the Neapolitan of Fred. Russo.

# CHAPTER XI

## ISCHIA

We spent a long summer month in Ischia — not as invalids in search of medicinal baths (for which, far back into antiquity, the island has been famous), but for the pure enjoyment of its beauty, of a wilder and less populated kind than elsewhere about Naples, and much less visited. It is a veritable wilderness of vine-yards along which the goatherds drive their timid beasts, while under the trembling shade figures sit and plait long ropes of coloured straws from morn till night. Before coming to Ischia I never realised that vines were capable of scenting the air with such real fragrance. They bear here grapes of a deep red (or "nero," as it is called), producing a wine so dark that it is chiefly used as colouring for other wines, finding, therefore, a very ready market. The unfermented juice is so rich with body and tannin that it is even possible to use it as ink. The whole island is more or less covered with these beautiful vineyards, pale early in the spring, but black with heavy clusters before the vintage ; and under their leaves the usually road-bound

FORIO, ISCHIA

Behind the town rise the slopes of the extinct volcano
of Epomeo.

*forestieri* are free to roam, with a delight in the contact with nature which the peasant probably never knows.

The tragedy of a quarter of a century ago impoverished Ischia, but saved it from the innovating disfigurements of modern life. Of what other spot round the coast can it be more truly said that hardly a building in it is ugly—that no appalling hotel stands as a kind of heliograph to fascinate all eyes ? Of Ischia this may be said in all truth. The island is wholly and rarely beautiful—a spot to tarry in with delight and to leave with regret.

Walks off the beaten tracks are not so easy to find round Naples as might be imagined. In Capri you must go up hill or down. At Sorrento the lack of walks is proverbial. At Amalfi hundreds of steep mountain steps must be faced before a walking level can be found. But in Ischia not only is there the ascent of Epomeo to be made, but also the poderes and woods that clothe the sides of the great mountain are exquisite haunts for the active pedestrian ; nor are they difficult or fatiguing climbs that require a Teutonic get-up of alpine hat and feather and heavy stick, as so many simple walks in Capri seem to need ; rather they are little country paths under the olive and oak trees where no soul passes save the woodcutters shunting felled boughs from ledge to ledge, or a woman singing to herself and child as she runs lightly past with bare feet. If we follow the vineyards up the mountain slopes, caverns are seen cut deep into the rocks, cool wine-cellars which were at one time in use in many wine-growing parts of Italy, though the custom has almost disappeared. Here and there in overgrown paths we come across tangled trails of blackberries as in an English lane; but nobody plucks them. If the Greeks in ages past considered them as a preventive for some of their ailments the Italian peasant to-day despises them utterly.

Sometimes, after solitary climbing, voices will break the stillness, and a group is seen seated on the threshold of some tiny dwelling—a woman plaiting red and green baskets and fans, surrounded by half a dozen children and pigs, all laughing and grunting together in the hot sunshine. This straw work is the great industry of Ischia, though it is not so fine in quality as the Tuscan kind. A long golden-tinted straw is used; it bends pliably over the fingers, and is gathered from a plant grown in great quantities at Fontana, the village nearest to Epomeo. The peasants use also the grain as an article of food, crushing and preparing it in certain sauces known as "succo di ragout."

Before the earthquake of 1883 this straw industry, the headquarters of which are at Lacco Ameno, was carried on laboriously and in primitive fashion by only a few fisherfolk, and for the very smallest gains. But at that time there happened to be by chance in the island two ladies whose names are familiar all over Naples for their beneficent works—Signora Meuricoffre and the Duchessa di Ravaschieri.[1] Determined to

[1] The death of this lady took place last summer. Her life was devoted to philanthropy, and her loss is deeply felt in Naples. A fine portrait-bust of the Duchessa stands in the Filangieri Museum.

# Ischia

improve and encourage the industry they provided designs by Neapolitan artists, and took such interest in the workers and their work that the whole aspect of the wretched little village was transformed. But the Italian poor are the hardest people in the world to help. The strawplaiters of Ischia developed such feuds of jealousy, such rivalry among themselves, that their benefactresses finally withdrew in disgust. Since then the industry has remained stationary, for the people are too ignorant to develop anything new without help.

Nevertheless, the pretty if somewhat useless articles turned out find their way to all parts of the world. The women here plait straw much as women elsewhere knit, and the vast number of fans for which Ischia has long been known still justifies the old love song which runs—

> "Not so many fans they plait at Ischia,
> Nor strawberries ripe are gathered at Marano,
> Nor as many quails fly over Capri,
> Nor comes as much sweet buttermilk from Massa,
> Nor in the sea as many small fish lie—
> As from thy bright eyes wounding arrows fly."

Many are the quaint songs sung about the island in a dialect which has a softer intonation than that of Naples. Up the hillside songs are continually heard, one voice answering another—a custom which, save at Procida and a few other places, has vanished from most of the country about.

Peasant life seems a simple enough thing all over the world ; but in the South it possesses a charm quite inseparable from the landscape. One is tempted to look upon it as just a part of the beautiful tree and plant life around, so perfectly do the Italian peasantry blend into the scenery of their country. They are, as it were, impregnated with sunlight and warmth. Their hair is sun-stained ; their skin sun-browned ; the uncovered necks of the women are burnt to cherry colour; their eyes are black as night. Just as in the North inclement weather makes an outdoor life one of endurance and of effort, in the South constant sunshine has fitted the peasant to the soil with a simplicity which makes their lives akin to the growth of southern plants that ripen rapidly, are made their use of, and die.

How curious it is that round Naples there are spots which may be said to produce a monotony of types and of intellect which never change with the changing times—a sameness which makes one feel that it is indeed a fiction that attributes to climate a direct influence upon the imagination. In this volcanic soil are all the elements which might, one would imagine, produce excitable and exalted minds ; yet it is only as we approach the foot of Vesuvius and its active fires that the " types volcanic " are to be found. Beyond, save in rare instances, all is monotony, unproductive and dead.

The Ischian, though less sophisticated than even the Caprian, is a prey to the vice of gambling, and plays with a persistent regularity which keeps the peasantry in a condition of abject poverty. Hundreds of francs are lost weekly by the poor in the Lottery ; and when it is remembered that this sum is principally subscribed

VIEW OF FORIO, ISLAND OF ISCHIA

Taken from the Torrione, home of the Neapolitan
sculptor, Giovanni Maltese.

by those who earn but a few francs in wages, and have often large families to support, the misery in which a large proportion struggle on is easily understood. The poorer the player, the higher the play—is as a motto all over the South.

Considering the kind of engrained evils against which the Italian poor have to contend, one is more than ever convinced that no change of Government, no increase of trade and lowering of taxes, no bettered sanitary conditions, really touch the evils at the root. Education, and that alone, is needed—not direct lessons against the folly of the Lottery, against superstitious faith, against theft and begging and all the Camorristic practices dear to them, but that simple compulsory schooling which clears the cobwebs from a man's mind and teaches him to think. The educated classes who play weekly in the Lottery do so, after all, with their eyes open ; but the poor are the victims of ignorance, their worst foe ; and in spite of all the advertised improvements of Naples — the schools, charities, and what not—the fact remains that the poorer working - classes are still bringing up their families without education of any kind.

The Ischian women seem more intelligent than the men. They answer questions readily and clearly, and have good business heads ; but this fact may strike the stranger just because all the ablest men emigrate now, and rarely return. It is quite out of the common to find any women among the peasants who have no husband, brother, or son abroad. Many of the men go to

# Naples

America or to the Cape. A few even go to over-crowded London, to hawk goods about the streets and carry on in fog and cold the traditional life of their sunny country. "You are English, 'gnorsi; but England may be a little country. My son is in London —a land so big that it must be very far away," said one woman to me.

A certain pathos attaches to Ischia as a consequence of the earthquake which left such calamity behind it. There is no doubt that the generality of tourists have been frightened away from the island, though there is no more ground for alarm here than elsewhere round the Neapolitan " crater "—indeed, much less. There is a great difference between an earthquake and the settlement of earth, since the first is as much of an omen for the future as the latter is comparatively a safeguard. The disaster of 1883 was so local that the guardian of Etna, Professor Silvestri, failed to detect any especial disturbances in his instruments at Catania, and the fissure in the crater was so minute that the gas (to quote an authority) was seen only in the imagination of some, and was nothing but the dust raised by the breeze at those points where the mountain was fissured and the detached masses fell at the last shock. Epomeo may be called practically extinct as long as the fumes rise from the mouth of Vesuvius, the active outlet, as it has ever been, of all the forces which lie beneath the Phlegrean fields and the volcanic islands round Naples. The disaster of Casamicciola is believed to have been due to an explosion of gases which might have happened

206

CHURCH OF S. PIETRO, ISCHIA

as easily in several other parts of the Neapolitan coast.

Nevertheless, the fact remains that Ischia was ruined not only by the disaster itself, but also by the widespread terror left in the public mind. The once gay centre of the Italian summer season, the pleasure-seat of the Bourbons among the vines which once brought in a round addition to their revenue, fell back into the old-time poverty.

But a better fate awaits it. New hotels are springing up, and its springs are as miraculous as ever. If fewer pleasure-seekers find their way to it, there is still a courageous and cosmopolitan assembly to be found with each summer, facing recklessly the volcanic dangers in which they firmly believe for the sake of that health without which life is not worth having. From early morn, during the summer months, the procession to the Baths begins, a few starting off on foot, though it requires a superhuman effort to face the hill in the sweltering heat. By luncheon time the mud is washed off, and conversation begins. The talk varies little with the days of the week, always ending with the remark, "It's wonderful! I feel another creature." And indeed it is quite remarkable to watch those who arrived decrepit with rheumatism able to walk off at the end of the season. It makes one almost regret having no illness at all in a spot where the remedy is one so enjoyable as sitting in hot mud and discussing it afterwards with one's friends.

The bathing society in the hotel was very amusing.

# Naples

There were a few English. A Swedish lady, whose cure consisted not only of mud ablutions, but also of a self-originated diet of hard nuts and milk, over which her doctor, figuratively, wept in despair. There was also a German blonde who, between every meal, slept with her head upon the dining-room table, to the great confusion of the waiters ; and in one corner a typical Neapolitan bourgeois family sat, who seemed to grow daily in size, as all fat people do. But foreign "types" rarely fit into a landscape harmoniously, and when thinking of Ischia the mind's eye sees the peasant life only—the dark Eastern faces of the girls as they pass by bearing the classic pitcher on their heads ; little groups of dirty children under the shade of flowering oleanders bright with double flowers ; goats, absurdly clad donkeys, labourers resting upon the wayside and devouring neatly peeled Indian figs ; and across the sea the continually changing sun effects upon the water.

It is a picture little changed, I imagine, since when, a century ago, Lamartine visited Ischia in his happy married life, in love with life and nature and disdainful of probable earthquakes. He was one of the very few who have known how to gather inspiration from the island's beauty ; and here he composed in his sober middle age that romance, every page of which glows with passionate youth and poetry. But the novels of the early nineteenth century are little read now, and the age of the Romanticists which grew, not only from the art galleries, but also from the real beauty and sentiment of Italian landscape, has long passed.

Ischia, like all volcanic regions, has a kind of exotic charm. Fruits grow with wild luxuriance, though for commercial purposes the vine is now taking the place of many other kinds. Pears, loquats or medlars, peaches (very hard, but ripe, though one feels they should not be so), figs and prickly pears, limes and the famous red cherries of Casamicciola—all grow freely. Mulberry trees abound, though continued lopping of the leaves for the silk-worms destroys the fruit. Of flowers the commonest are the wild cyclamen, the arbutus, the richly-scented large violets, and mountain wild-flowers growing up the sides of Epomeo, the names of which I do not know. The Italian peasant, when asked the name of any flower, makes always the same answer, " Una pianta qualunque." Along the roadsides are oleander trees, which spring up rapidly, and as rapidly die. It is characteristic of the planting of trees in the South that when they *are* planted, unenduring and comparatively worthless kinds are chosen. But tree-planting and cutting is to-day a sore subject in Italy from north to south, and the country may be said still to await an Italian Evelyn to discourse on forest trees with the same success that such argument produced long ago in England.[1]

The ruined dwellings about the island remain just as they collapsed in 1885, in the midst of heaps of

[1] The law, forbidding the cutting down of a tree without the planting of three in its place, is rarely put into effect.

débris. Casamicciola is not unlike a tiny Pompeii, with the rosy bright dabs of vermilion paint which Italians of all ages have loved still clinging to the walls, and the sunshine and lizards sparkling in the courtyards. It might have happened a thousand years ago as easily as yesterday, and only little details remind us of its proximity to our own times. "That was my home," said our driver as we passed up the hill from Casamicciola, and he pointed to a ruined dwelling. "My little boy was buried under the ruins." He spoke as though the tragedy had but just happened, for Italians love nothing if not their children; had it been his wife he might have forgotten the fact.

Ruins mark also the mountain path from Casamicciola to Forio. On one side stands the old Cathedral, open now to the day, and far more beautiful, no doubt, in its dilapidated condition than when its pretentious façade hid the line of hills behind. There is no money to rebuild it; when, indeed, will there ever be? This walk, skirting along the beautiful view of sea and sky, with the dim outline of Procida behind us, and stretches of vines between us and the shore, is one of the loveliest on the island. It leads down into the little town of Lacco Ameno, with its golden beach, and strange trunk of stone rising from the sea. Here it was that the dead saint was washed up in the past; and the Festival of S. Restituta has lost less of its old time simplicity than have most of the native customs round the island. It may be likened to the Festival of Montevergine of Naples, both fêtes acting

A STREET IN CASAMICCIOLA, ISCHIA

as an inducement to whole families from all parts to join in its celebration and to have at least one day's outing in the year. Just as the marriage contracts of the Neapolitan peasants once included participation in the Festival of Piedigrotta among the wife's rights, so the Ischian women claimed a right to be escorted by their husbands to Lacco in the month of May. No doubt the custom had a singular importance in the days when women were subjected to an almost Eastern mode of indoor life.

S. Restituta possesses untold wealth in the way of jewels and costly offerings of the past centuries, besides many humble gifts of the poor. Some years ago these possessions were stolen by a poor fisherman, and hidden in the sand to await an opportunity of being transferred to Naples and sold. But fear at his evil deed tormented the thief; and he ran away without his riches, which were happily discovered and restored. The minds of the poor, however, were much disturbed at the occurrence, and one peasant was heard to say, mournfully and with a certain justice, to the saint's image in the church, "Blessed Saint, if you cannot look after your possessions better than that, I, for one, will certainly give you nothing more."

This is not the only festival of Ischia. Following the road from Lacco, we reach Forio, where there is a procession of its patron saint, S. Vito, in the summer. But to those who remember this festival some thirty years ago, with its quaint costumes, and the perfume of broom and lavender and pinks floating

sweetly through church and streets, the affair of to-day
seems like all the other countless noisy fêtes of Naples.
There are the fireworks, the gaudy and tasteless
decorations, the discordant town bands. It is only on
Easter day that the century-old ceremony which may
yet be seen in many parts of Italy remains unchanged.
Between eleven and midday a dense crowd collects on
either side of the principal street leading past the
church of S. Maria di Tareto. Along this road, borne
on men's shoulders, two painted wooden statues slowly
advance. They represent the figures of St. John and
the Virgin Mary, whose face is covered by a thick
black veil. Opposite to them comes the Brotherhood
of S. Maria Visitapoveri in long white surplice gowns ;
and in their midst is carried a large golden angel ; and
last of all a figure of Christ, risen and triumphant. At
a given signal the standard of the Brotherhood is
waved aside ; the Christ remains stationary ; and the
angel, after bending before Him in salute, turns and is
carried at full speed through the passage left by the
spectators to announce to the Virgin that her Son is
risen. The Virgin refuses to believe, and the Angel
returns sadly to the Christ to tell Him of his unsuccess.
Again sent to the Virgin, but all in vain, he again
retires ; and yet again is sent upon his urgent mission
to the holy Mother, who now begins, half in doubt, to
move slowly forward. Joyfully the angel reports this
to the Son, who once more sends him to encourage
St. John and His Mother, both of whom finally believe,
and rush forward to see the great truth for themselves.

EVENING UPON THE BEACH OF THE
MARINA OF ISCHIA

# Ischia

During this curious bit of Miracle Play, the people continue to sing loudly the "Regina Coeli"; and at the meeting of Mother and Son the veil of the Virgin drops, pigeons and small birds are allowed to fly around, from every window and roof wafers float down, and from the Campanili the bells announce that the ceremony is over. Then gradually the mass of human beings in their bright holiday garb seems to melt away like a dissolving kaleidoscope, and the streets resume their sleepy character.

The contributions to cover the expenses of the religious festivals in Ischia are subscribed by emigrant Italians in America and at the Cape, but mostly by the peasants themselves, who would fain avert all evils that menace their land—plague, pestilence, and earthquake—by insuring themselves, their vineyards, houses, boats, and fish, against every possible calamity, arguing that should the ground of Ischia quake again S. Vito, if handsomely fêted, should save at least a portion. It is their investment, and they believe implicitly in the interest it gives.

The festival of Forio has gained greatly in importance of late years, owing to the energy of a town official who encourages the people to subscribe generously, and has even persuaded the naval authorities to lend the presence of a man-of-war for the great occasion. A year or two ago there were no fewer than four warships, English and Italian, anchored in the Bay of Forio!

There is a quaint fashion here attached to the use of

eggs at Easter. On Palm Sunday it is the custom for a young affianced girl to send a gift of a hundred and one eggs and a branch of olive to her lover ; and on the day of S. Restituta, May 17, the grateful lover sends her in return twelve pounds of *torrone*, a sweet-meat peculiar to Italy, made of honey and almonds, and harder than most stones. A young fellow asked this favour of an egg one day as he looked up at the window of a mischievous girl. "Ma certo," she answered, and, fetching one fresh and raw, broke it neatly over his face. But far from discouraging him, this proceeding filled him with such hope and determination that they were speedily married, and have now a merry family of children, both parents probably believing it was one of the substantial sources of their prosperity.

Some one has said that Forio is Turneresque ; and indeed there is something of the idealism of the great painter in the broad sweep of its white towers and houses straggling into the sea from the distant slopes of the mountain behind, on which clouds rest softly, or float away like a breath from the barren crater. The Cistercian Convent, the Moorish towers, the white fishing houses, the peaceful bay lapping their feet,—all show with wonderful distinctness in the lucid air. Farther on the road dwindles away, and finally stops on the eminence of S. Angelo. Far away over the slopes of vineyards a narrow neck of land runs into a jutting promontory forming twin bays to right and left and crowned with peasants' huts all the way. And as the night falls lights from these humble dwellings twinkle like stars above the sea.

If the streets of Forio seem at times monotonous and lacking in life, it is because all the animation has bubbled over on to the beautiful beach, where knots of fishermen, children, and idlers are lying on the sands, gesticulating. Two towers dominate the town, and one, a curious relic of mediæval times, and still almost perfect, stands not far from the seashore, and is now the dwelling of an Ischian sculptor and his English wife, herself a clever aquarellist. This sturdy monument of the past has been adapted with artistic taste by the present owners into a modern dwelling. Flowers grow all about it ; oleander and olive trees shade the garden ; a vine is trellised over the steps ; roses, velvety honey flowers, passion flowers, and red pomegranates, clematis and geraniums, beautify it ; and it is wonderful how all this mass of flowering vegetation resists the sea-spray which from time to time washes over it. On the little terrace stand some fine specimens of the great oil jars, disused now on the island, since oil was found to pre-serve better in tin cans. A more romantic home cannot be imagined ; and how beautiful is it as the day falls and the glowing sunfire lights the stern gray of its turreted walls ! One must see Forio at sunset to realise its beauty. Nowhere in all this region are the glories of the setting sun more amply reflected. The little bay of Forio is before us ; to the left stretches the breakwater ; and the Franciscan Convent crowns the Punto Caruso. The distant outline of the island of Ponza shows but a delicate ridge of deep blue as the sun sinks, and reminds us of the first view that Ulysses had of his native land :

"It seemed like a shield in the violet sea."

The Ischian side of the island is less idyllic in that it is less wild and more inhabited. A long dust-white road leads from Casamicciola to Ischia, along which in the cool of the evening are to be seen all the utterly dilapidated vehicles that can be hired, filled with summer visitors. Men and women laden with straw wares pass us on the way,—girls with jars underneath their arms and on their heads as well, and friendly peasants, who attach themselves to the solitary foreigner on foot, and never leave him as long as he consents to let them make his life a burden.

As we approach the town there is a lovely stretch of beach along which may sometimes be seen a magnificent peacock spreading its plumage, dark and glowing against the blue of the sea. Ischia has as oriental a taste in its animals as in its vegetation. Monkeys sported here in the past, it is said ; and peacocks are a favourite trophy of the returned emigrant.

At the end of the street of Ischia, familiar Neapolitan perfumes greet us with that old welcome which, in the flowery country round Casamicciola, we had almost forgotten. The drive goes but a little farther, passing on the left the beautiful and now deserted home of an Englishman—perhaps the most romantic of all foreign dwellings about Naples—till it comes in view of the wonderful old castle of the Pascara, jutting out into the

sea, a veritable sentinel of nature, as it was indeed a sentinel of the past. The interior of its courts are now filled with hundreds of ratskins drying in the sun—the only modern use these stern walls have succumbed to.

To us it would seem too severe a ruin to conjure up other than feelings of gloom ; but in the days of the happy lovers, D'Avolos and his young bride Vittoria, the bare rocks were covered more luxuriantly than now, and this quarter of the island was the centre of all that was noble and cultured of that time. It was the spot where Vittoria Colonna wrote the greater part of her tender and feminine poetry, bequeathing to Ischia the echo of a poet's name, though not her birthplace.

# CHAPTER XII

## CAPRI

" Far in the distance amidst the languor of waves, lies Capri,
Swift vessels pass to and fro, the sailors swing to the masthead,
While the light bark beguiles to the breast of the saffron ocean."
(Translation from the German of Von Platen.)

HOWEVER familiar we may be with the Bay of Naples
in general, it is a complete revelation to land at Capri.
This island is a world apart from the peninsula with
which, in the unknown past, it must once have been
a whole. Three miles of sea have sufficed to create
another people, another atmosphere, another scenery
and climate. One is struck on landing with a complete change in the surrounding elements, human and
cosmical. A sense of sculpturesque solidity is received,
and insensibly one thinks of stern and sphinx-like
forms. It is indeed the form of this island which is
its especial charm. Ruskin felt it when, grievously
disappointed with his first view of Naples, "ready
to cry like a girl" with the bad roads and miserable
weather, he first caught sight of the beautiful shapes
of Monte S. Angelo and Capri. The rocks seem

STREET IN CAPRI

# Capri

chiselled as by some great master. Surely a statuette of Capri, delicately modelled and true to nature, would be a perfect work of art?

On landing from the boat, the sturdy, almost masculine types of the peasant women who crowd about the quay to unload the passengers' heavy luggage are a sight never to be forgotten. How unlike the eastern and somewhat melancholy types of Ischia or the women of Sorrento and Amalfi! Tall, powerful, somewhat boisterous in health and spirits, with a dash of savagery, they are the ideal mothers of an island home. Caprian women have an apparent dignity of their own, a quality which is far from common in a country where, as Madame de Stael remarks, dignity more than other qualities is lacking. We are in a land where the aristocracy of the peasant is the only aristocracy. Ischia has had its feudal days, its old mediæval traditions ; Capri none. With the death of Tiberius began more or less the unmomentous existence which the island has since maintained. Its legends of tyranny and dissolute romance died away, and with the centuries Capri became famous only for its calm peasant life and the industry and morality of its inhabitants. Let us hope such a tradition may outlive even our degenerate age. The Italian noblesse have never sought a footing here ; and, curiously enough, its beauty and immunity from volcanic dangers have never attracted Italians. It is the northern races who are gradually colonising the island, and slowly but surely blending their language and characteristics with those of the natives. The Teuton, not beautiful himself, has an unerring eye for the beautiful in nature. He loves, too, ground where the traces of Roman days linger in the soil, and, as if a passion for contrast filled him with a grotesque delight, will erect architectural monstrosities in spots which not only nature but the ruins of great ages have idealised.

Unfortunately, in Italy the new element quickly destroys the old, and customs and costumes disappear rapidly. Only some among the fisher women and lads wear still their charming red "tammies," and the youths discard these, appearing on every possible festive occasion in hard black hats. The transformation these changes of dress occasion is quite particularly trying to the artist's mind. One painter who had made a successful study of a boy in his "tammie," and felt inspired to make another, looked up her model at a festa ; and there he was, hideous to behold, in shining black head-gear.

"No, I'll not have you again," she remarked in real disgust. "But, Signora," he said in amazement, and pointing to the lining of his hat, "was it not made in Germany ? "

We had a long talk about the island with an Italian artist, a Roman, who has made Capri his home for many years. "You have no idea," he said, "how utterly primitive a being is the native of Capri. In the scale of mental and moral development he seems to me a far more rudimentary creature than the South Italian peasant of the mainland. His ignorance, as far as education goes, has been accentuated by the narrow

# Capri

limitations proverbial to the islander, and a certain poverty of ideas which ensues from being out of all touch with the people of the continent. I have lived here many years and find it difficult to bring up my children so as to prevent them from falling to the level of the contadini about. The late Herr Krupp, the great German manufacturer, had some excellent schemes for founding schools in the island, which would have been admirable if he had lived to carry them out, and if the narrow sectarian politics of the place had not thrown obstacles in his way. He had set himself a stiff task, for nothing is more difficult than to help a people among whose lower class reigns a crass ignorance, while the petty bourgeoisie are engaged in constant political feuds. Unhappily, he died before seeing any of his philanthropic ideals realised."

Meanwhile the great beauty of the island has drawn hither foreigners from all parts of the world, who have erected villas on many a lovely slope, some of them full of charm in an architecture which seems to have developed naturally from the peasants' houses. The gleaming whiteness of their walls in the rarified air of Capri gives a certain oriental brilliance which one meets nowhere else.

Drive down from the Quisisana to the Piccola Marina if you wish to see a thoroughly characteristic bit of Capri. The road, built at great expense by Herr Krupp, was left not quite finished at his death : so you must make up your mind to be sadly jolted on the way down by the unrolled macadam : for the town authorities have not as yet had the enterprise to complete the splendid work of their benefactor. On the right-hand side one passes the villa of the talented painter, Lovatti, built with a beautiful loggia and pergola in the style of a Pompeian house. Farther down, that magnificent group of rocks known as the Faraglioni appears in all its glory. Turner caught well the spirit of this side of nature in the azure distance of that masterpiece, "Ulysses deriding Polyphemus." Finally, the road ends at the Piccola Marina. What a quaint bit of fisherman nature is this secluded spot! The rocks about are delightfully grouped, forming tiny arches and promontories, as in some fairy scene in a scene-painter's dream. Here are the "seats of living rock" of the *Æneid*, and it would be difficult to imagine anything more pregnant of the mythical sea-roving stories of the ancients.

It is over a century since Germanic influence began to take root in the island. A friend, a German himself, advised us by no means to go to Capri, because, said he, "my compatriots have ruined the place"; and indeed it is the fashion among tourists to affirm that this is so. It seems to me, however, that nothing could be further from the truth. The Teutonic element in the little town of Capri itself has introduced a régime of order and cleanliness which one does not find in any other South Italian town; and if the local colour has been effaced in places, it is perhaps compensated for by the model of civilisation shown to the inhabitants.

I believe that it was the well-known poetic effusion

PEASANT GIRL OF CAPRI

# Capri

on Pagano's café that first attracted the general flow of German tourists to the island ; but the discovery of the Blue Grotto no doubt started popular interest in it. Kopisch, who first brought its beauty into notice, was not only an expert swimmer, but also a poet belonging to that brief period of Neapolitan history when Naples may be said to have struck a sudden fount of poesy,— when Von Platen and Leopardi were under the spell of this beautiful land.

The Blue Grotto is as mysterious in its beauty and history as it is in the effect it produces on many a visitor's mind. In spite of its wonderful properties of colour, the first impression is always one of disappointment. It is a scene which words have proved incapable of describing accurately, and artists cannot catch its values. Andersen wrote of it as in a dream, and the dream is so surpassingly beautiful that the reality seems more like a copy than the original. But the curious thing is that, though the Blue Grotto may seem to fall short of our expectations at the moment, when remembered the imagination colours it with just as brilliant hues, and we think of it always as a wonderful dream, just as Andersen did.

Every morning the sea in front of the cave is dotted with the tiny cockle-shell boats which came into use with its discovery. They bob about, waiting for the daily steamer loaded with sightseers, and for a brief half-hour the Blue Grotto is a veritable pandemonium. Let us wait till the last has pulled back towards the steamer, or towards the shore of the Marina, before

visiting it.  There is a pebbly bit of beach beneath the
Ruined Baths of Tiberius, and only ten minutes' distance
from the Grotto, where we can anchor our boat and
await the opportune moment.  A stout individual who
has spread bathing-towel and mat in the shade of a
rock, in anticipation of a plunge into the sparkling water
under the conditions that Walt Whitman has glorified,
glares at us furiously.  Such is life now, and one tourist
must hunt another from his lair like the wild beasts of
the forest.

All is quiet at last ; and we row round the jutting
rock to the entrance, lie flat in the boat, and pass
through the low aperture.

The world seems suddenly reversed, and the blue
sky lies beneath where but a second before green water
gleamed.  We can touch the thousand stars that break
over it as the oar moves.  The blue light which is
already familiar by hearsay before we see it does not
envelope : it only lies profoundly and deeply blue
below.  Above, all is shadow and darkness, and the
boat floats upon liquid as transparent as air and as
living as blue flame.  No other effect in nature has
ever been produced by so slight a cause.  Were the
level of the water lowered by even six feet, the rock
on the right of the entrance would remain some two
feet out of the sea, and the light entering through so
large an aperture would dissolve this fairy world.  Such
must have been the case in ancient times, no doubt ;
and this would account for the fact that no mention
is made of the phenomena.  That the sea has risen

# Capri

(or rather that the land has sunk) the coasts of Puzzoli and of Misena bear ample witness. That it is still sinking perhaps the Temple of Serapis will in its turn some day prove.

Another Grotto, still less easily accessible as yet to the ordinary tourist, has recently been discovered, and again by a German. The rocks that frown over the sea are gemmed with these translucent caves, lending something strangely unreal to their sternness—for that they are stern no one will deny. The hills around Athens have been spoken of as a chorus. I should be inclined to liken the majestic forms of Capri to the Protagonist of the drama. They frown, seeming to lament, their feet washed by the ever-murmuring sea like to some Prometheus.

But amid the smiling Nature of Capri it is only at moments that the extraordinary character of the mountain shapes takes the mind back to antiquity. Thrilling deliciously through the trees at sunrise and sunset is heard the song of birds—even the chirping of quails, which is so rarely heard now on the mainland, owing to their slaughter for food; those creatures, says the *Englishman in Italy*—

> "Whose heads—speckled white
> Over brown like a great spider's back,
> As I told you last night—
> Your mother bites off for her supper."

The cactus and the aloes spring from the bare earth. The vine winds up its high poles, or is festooned over the tiny pergolas. In the autumn groups sit under them, sorting out masses of prickly pears, separating into basketfuls the green from the black olives, or stringing together into ropes the small green tomatoes which will hang and ripen with time into scarlet on the sunny walls. Through dark doorways is seen the primitive crushing of the olives into wine, while the patient tread of horse or mule grinds round its wheel.

The gardens are bright with flowers. Blue convolvulus train up the tree-trunks or float over the walls with a strange growth of the trefoil and rounded leaf on a single stem. The purple mint, which is said by some to ward off mosquitoes—the peasant women use it to perfume their "boccato"—springs, as is its way, from the stoniest spots, and floods the air with sweetness. The scent, said to be partly due to camphor in the plant, can revive as well as delight. It is easy to understand why poets, even from classic times, have loved this humble flower, with its rock-coloured leafage, which throws out its entire fragrance even as the foot crushes it.

Here and there a wild flowering aloe rises like a slender wand across the sky from the midst of its withered leaves ; for the leaves of the common Italian aloe fade as the flower blooms. All this vegetation partakes of the pale tint of the rocks, and olive and aloe and cactus melt into the grays of the limestone. The dark and "dewless" cypress and the yew, which make such a note of contrast in the South, are absent here save in one garden mentioned elsewhere, and in their traditional home, the Campo Santo.

# Capri

"Both you two have
  Relation to the grave,"

writes Herrick ; but it was only the cypress which the
Romans dedicated to Pluto, as a funeral tree, believing
that when once cut it never grew again.

How curious is it that about all the luxuriant
vegetation and flora of Naples no legends linger !
Trees and flowers, so often enveloped with story in
the North, have here purely practical associations.
The spring bursts into flower without one of the old
customs with which the Romans welcomed it, dedicat-
ing the season to Flora and wearing in her honour
woven garlands of the blossoms with which she had
strewn the earth. In the native poetry of Naples
floral terms and similitudes are used only to draw
comparisons between them and the amorous feelings
of the people, and even these allusions are restricted to
three or four flowers and fruits—the rose, the cherry,
the pomegranate. I could give a hundred instances ;
but the two I choose are fair examples from the
Neapolitan :—

"Sweet as the cherry,
  Rosy as the pomegranate flower,
  Ah ! how that mouth o'erwhelms me
  With its witching power."

or—

"Look at this rose, just look at it,
  Soft as velvet, red as flame,
  How it resembles your pretty mouth
  Side by side the same." [1]

---

[1] Translations from the Neapolitan.

# Naples

No doubt the melodious quality in the names of flowers has played its part in dialect poetry, as elsewhere. The ugly Italian name for the cherry has, in dialect, been transformed into the soft-sounding " Cerase " and " Curvina," accounting somewhat for its constant poetic use about Naples, while of course the rose's name is the softest in sound of any plant. But ignorance of, and indifference to, flowers in general has played a part in limiting their floral vocabulary. The feeling for Nature has little inspired in it, nor does it seem to raise the ideals of the people in any way. We are in a country where the wearing of flowers is almost unknown. Even in Naples ladies rarely wear them, and such a fashion would be viewed as a mere frivolity.

But enough of roses and cherries, though in the early summer they force their beauty upon the senses.

> " It was the month of May, and in her lap
> Bunch by bunch the ripe red cherries fell;
> Sweet was the air, and all the garden lay
> Beneath the perfume of the roses' spell." [1]

In Capri, as elsewhere, are found the old towers of the middle ages. They were not buildings of any great importance, save for the purpose of watching the coast. Built in the very spots least able to resist the elements, it might be natural to suppose that they would have completely disappeared as their use declined. Yet they are still to be seen, sturdy and fantastic, sentinels lingering at their post. A fashion for buying, restoring, and living in them has spread very much of

[1] Translation from the Neapolitan of di Giacomo.

FISHER GIRL OF CAPRI

# Capri

late years. How curious is the need—is it decadent ?
— certain modern types of mind display of being
surrounded by old walls and ruins ! They gather a
veritable inspiration from the deserted dwellings of past
lives ; and the more " modern " is life in other respects,
the more does it draw intellectually on these mysterious
sentiments which, perhaps, were unknown in the days
when the ruined walls were new and firm.

In Capri one of these " torrione " can be seen from
a lovely point of view at Caprioli, hiding amid a gray
wilderness of olives far above the sea. Rescued from
threatened vandalism, it is now in the possession of
Dr. Munthé, the Swedish author of *Letters from a
Mourning City*, who first settled in the island years
before tourist elements and disfiguring architecture and
eccentric legends had destroyed its wild charm. It is
the natural lot of all of our day who love and covet
remote beauty in Nature to watch that charm dwindle
before encroaching civilisation. It is at least consoling
to think that perhaps even Tiberius in *his* day experi-
enced a foretaste of it, hunted from villa to villa up to
the heights of Anacapri.

The Podere of olives and orange-trees in the midst
of which stands this winter home is, I believe, the
largest in Capri. A long path bordered with rude
overgrown pillars leads to the tower, and on every side
beneath the trees the brown earth has been planted
with a wild growth of roses, free to grow whithersoever
they will unthreatened by gardener's laws : a Roman
rose garden, without the fastidious artificiality of Roman

days. This delight in gardens without gardeners is but one of the many possibilities that the South gives us—a gift in itself.

The interior of the tower is still more strange than beautiful. It is too distinct and personal for strict perfection, too much stamped with the eccentric character of its owner ; but in this lies its very charm. All connoisseurs collect in somewhat the same manner, but this tiny interior is more than a mere catalogue of objects. There are, for example, ample signs that this collector not only loves his gems, but also understands their setting. Even the enchanting views from the tower are framed in windows of exquisite Byzantine workmanship, windows that give æsthetic delight to gaze from.

Far above, overlooking Anacapri and the whole superb view, stands another dwelling, a summer villa, half Roman, half Byzantine. The walls, inside and out, are pure dead white, contrasting with the deep green that looks in from every window. This villa is a museum of rare objects—a lived-in museum with just the touch of sadness which collected and defaced treasures must possess. Here is a colossal head of marble which the owner saw one day lying under the transparent sea. Here are columns restored from the waters of the Bay of Naples—that Bay which has washed over untold wealth of Greco - Roman days. Byzantine mosaics are inserted into the walls, and in the garden are old sarcophagi, antique time - changed statuary, half hidden under the vegetation.

IN THE VILLA MUNTHÉ, ANACAPRI

A museum of rare objects of art.

# Capri

Was it one of the villas of Tiberius? Dr. Munthé claims the possibility at least. He believes that upon the beautiful little terrace the tyrant was pacing to and fro, tremulous with a forewarning of bad tidings, when the news of Christ's death reached him. There are many traces of the age of the villa's foundations, and a skeleton biting still the coin which marked him as a pagan may be seen in its hollow at the villa.

In the garden may be seen a long avenue of tiny cypresses, the only specimens of the tree on the island.

There is still carried out on New Year's Eve at Anacapri an old custom which must surely have originated in some pre-nervous period of man's existence. The native lads of the place, armed with primitive musical instruments and a large upright log, enter the houses of their various friends and "plant" the happiness of the inmates for the coming year by thumping the log in the middle of the floor for what would seem to our ears an eternity. A monotonous chant is kept up during the whole performance. As to the Caprian's idea of music, it is certainly curious, among the inevitable changes resulting from foreign influence, how little of German music and song has penetrated to Capri. Never was there a more silent isle—not a guitar, hardly a mandoline, even in the barbers' salons, where these instruments are usually so much in request. Only the singing and twittering of birds at sunrise and sunset is heard.

Speaking of birds, the great Easter Eve celebration on the Saturday at mid-day is wonderful to witness. At the sound of the Gloria hundreds of little birds are suddenly let free from baskets, pockets, and the hot hands of many children, adding a wild chirp of delight to the ringing and clanging of the bells.

The life of Capri is distinctly an outdoor one. The air, surcharged with ozone, fills the body with a delightful energy. Ravenous hunger makes every meal-time a delight—even luncheon-time I might say, for it is then that Capri is stormed with hungry visitors from all parts of the world—American women with long floating veils ; Neapolitan families, who care not the least for the "sights" but dearly love an excursion ; German couples, absorbed and happy ; and a few, but very few, English, and those mostly honeymoon couples. This feeding hour is unlike anything of the kind elsewhere. The rush and hurry, the indecent haste to be fed, followed by a sleepy and replenished lingering over the tables, seems to repeat itself day after day with unchanging regularity. But in spite of these too human surroundings, there is something so truly exhilarating in the delicious Caprian climate, that, whatever else Capri may lack, let us at least glorify it for this one solid virtue which makes life so well worth living.

For my part, I believe that air scented with flowers is more of a cure for mind and body than many an advertised tonic.

It was while we were at Capri that we met a Neapolitan lady who was there with her children for the bathing. Along with other hotel acquaintances

# Capri

she was on the best of terms with a very tall thin foreigner in spectacles. When one of her children fell ill, he gave her a simple remedy; but, as is so often the case, the child persisted in carrying through its illness in its own fashion, and promptly developed fever. This elicited further offers of help; but the lady received them in almost trembling fear, turned pale, and, excusing herself, hastened away. It was the old story of the jettatura. Poor man! He had all the attributes supposed to accompany the ill, and the lady herself, a Neapolitan, was certainly to blame in not having noticed them sooner. To be tall, meagre in body, and to wear blue spectacles, is almost always the outward and visible form of the inward sin. It was but last summer that I read in one of the daily newspapers the description of just such a person who had lately landed at Naples, and was declared to have brought with him the particularly bad weather that happened to be raging at the time.

That an individual may have the Evil Eye is believed all over Italy, but the peculiarly terrible belief in its heredity seems to be purely Neapolitan. One of the oldest and noblest families in Naples is said to possess this incurable taint, and that to such a degree that the family name has been changed, and a member of it, a Neapolitan poet, has left behind him less of the poet's name than this legend of the jettatura, which has made him the hero of a well-known French romance. It is only a wonder that the family should still exist and not have died out, for marriages

into it were made with the greatest difficulty, and
S. Catarine *coiffés* many of the daughters for no other
reason.  The belief in the jettatura is much more
noticeable among the educated than among the ignorant.
Nor must it be forgotten that France, a country which
is considered as in every way more enlightened than
Italy, embittered the life of a great musician for no
other reason.

Some years ago Capri was a great centre for the
tarantella ; but the dance has now grown artificial and
cosmopolitanised both here and at Sorrento.  Little
of the old wild spirit of its origin can now be traced
in this, the only relic of the mania for dancing which
the bite of the harmless tarantula spider was said to
have spread over Europe in the Middle Ages.  The
following poem hardly describes the tame performance
which is now to be seen :—

"Listen !  The castanets of yon happy pair
Are striking loudly together, and now begins
The Tarantella, Bacchantic, luxuriant dance !
See how the young girl moves as lightly as air ;
And the handsome youth, how swiftly he leaps and spins,
And turns with the rhythm, stamping with fiery glance !
And now he flings at the fair girl's heart, a rose.
But all the covetous fire is checked in his eyes,
Tamed by her softly commanding mien, maiden wise
In her country's restraint.  Oh, fortunate land !
For Nature withholds it nought from her magic wand,
Not e'en the calm reserve that the North never knows." [1]

I sometimes think that form is more distinctly

[1] Translated from the original of Von Platen.

**VILLA DUBUFFE**

Home of the celebrated French painter.

# Capri

remembered than the changing colour of Nature upon which the eye can never gaze sufficiently long to be wholly master of it. Homes of rock and stone get a kind of grip on the memory, a mastery, as it were, through their brute strength, when the purely lovely fades away like a dream.

As we approach Naples, and the melting colours of the Bay once more envelop us, when, looking back, Capri has faded into a transparent fresco upon the horizon, the mind's eye still sees the great outline of rock, the sphinxes of limestone that sink into the sea. What contrasts of beauty are there in this land! A mere glance seems to separate the majestic from the languid, the stern from the gentle forms of Nature, and we know not which to think the most lovely.

> " Il faut dans ce bas monde aimer beaucoup de choses,
> Pour savoir après tout ce qu'on aime le mieux."

THE END

*Printed by* R. & R. CLARK, LIMITED, *Edinburgh.*

# BLACK'S BEAUTIFUL BOOKS
## ALL WITH FULL-PAGE ILLUSTRATIONS IN COLOUR
### THE 20s. NET SERIES

By Post, Price 20s. 6d.    Size 9 × 6¼ ins.

**Algeria and Tunis**
Painted and Described by FRANCES E. NESBITT. 70 Full-Page Illustrations in Colour.

**The Alps**
Described by SIR MARTIN CONWAY. Painted by A. D. M'CORMICK. 70 Full-Page Illustrations in Colour.

**Ancient Tales and Folk=Lore of Japan**
By R. GORDON SMITH, F.R.G.S. Painted by Japanese Artists. 57 Full-Page Illustrations in Colour.

**Australia**
Painted by PERCY F. S. SPENCE. Described by FRANK FOX. 75 Full-Page Illustrations in Colour.

**Belgium**
Painted by A. FORESTIER. Described by G. W. T. OMOND. 77 Full-Page Illustrations in Colour.

**Birds of Britain**
By J. LEWIS BONHOTE, M.A., F.L.S., F.Z.S. 100 Full-Page Illustrations in Colour, selected by H. E. DRESSER.

**Birket Foster**
By H. M. CUNDALL, I.S.O., F.S.A. 100 Full-Page Illustrations (over 70 in Colour) and many Sketches in the Text.

**Burma**
Painted and Described by R. TALBOT KELLY, R.B.A. 75 Full-Page Illustrations in Colour.

**Cambridge**
By M. A. R. TUKER. Painted by WILLIAM MATTHISON. 77 Full-Page Illustrations in Colour.

**Canada**
Painted by T. MOWER MARTIN, R.C.A. Described by WILFRED CAMPBELL. 76 Full-Page Illustrations in Colour.

**The Channel Islands**
Painted by HENRY B. WIMBUSH. Described by EDITH F. CAREY. 76 Full-Page Illustrations in Colour.

**The Clyde**
Painted by MARY Y. HUNTER and J. YOUNG HUNTER. Described by NEIL MUNRO. 67 Full-Page Illustrations in Colour.

**Constantinople**
Painted by WARWICK GOBLE. Described by PROF. ALEXANDER VAN MILLINGEN, D.D. 63 Full Page Illustrations in Colour.

**From Damascus to Palmyra**
By JOHN KELMAN, M.A., D.D. Painted by MARGARET THOMAS. 70 Full-Page Illustrations in Colour.

**Egypt**
Painted and Described by R. TALBOT KELLY, R.B.A. 75 Full-Page Illustrations in Colour.

**Egyptian Birds**
Painted and Described by CHARLES WHYMPER, F.Z.S., B.O.U. 51 Full-Page Illustrations in Colour.

**Happy England**
By HELEN ALLINGHAM, R.W.S. Text by MARCUS B. HUISH. 80 Full-Page Illustrations in Colour. (Size 9½ × 7 ins.)

**The Rivers and Streams of England**
Painted by SUTTON PALMER. Described by A. G. BRADLEY. 75 Full-Page Illustrations in Colour.

**English Costume**
By DION CLAYTON CALTHROP. 73 Full-Page Illustrations in Colour and numerous Sketches in the Text.

**The English Lakes**
Painted by A. HEATON COOPER. Described by WILLIAM T. PALMER. 75 Full-Page Illustrations in Colour.

**Essex**
Painted by BURLEIGH BRUHL, R.B.A. Described by A. R. HOPE MONCRIEFF. 75 Full-Page Illustrations in Colour.

**Florence and some Tuscan Cities**
Painted by COLONEL R. C. GOFF. Described by MRS. GOFF. 75 Full-Page Illustration in Colour.

**The Flowers and Gardens of Japan**
Painted by ELLA DU CANE. Described by FLORENCE DU CANE. 50 Full-Page Illustrations in Colour.

**The Lake of Geneva**
Painted by J. HARDWICKE LEWIS and MAY HARDWICKE LEWIS. Described by FRANCIS GRIBBLE. 60 Full-Page Illustrations in Colour.

**Greece**
Painted by JOHN FULLEYLOVE, R.I. Described by REV. J. A. M'CLYMONT, M.A., D.D. 75 Full-Page Illustrations in Colour.

**Kate Greenaway**
By M. H. SPIELMANN, F.S.A., and G. S. LAYARD. 75 Full-Page Illustrations (51 in Colour) and numerous Illustrations in the Text.

**Hampshire**
Painted by WILFRID BALL, R.E. Described by REV. TELFORD VARLEY. 75 Full-Page Illustrations in Colour.

**Holland**
By NICO JUNGMAN. Text by BEATRIX JUNGMAN. 75 Full-Page Illustrations in Colour.

**The Holy Land**
Painted by JOHN FULLEYLOVE, R.I. Described by REV. JOHN KELMAN, M.A., D.D. 93 Full-Page Illustrations, mostly in Colour.

**Hungary**
Painted by MR. AND MRS. ADRIAN STOKES. Described by ADRIAN STOKES, A.R.A. 75 Full-Page Illustrations in Colour.

**India**
By MORTIMER MENPES. Text by FLORA A. STEEL. 75 Full-Page Illustrations in Colour.

**Ireland**
Painted by FRANCIS S. WALKER, R.H.A. Described by FRANK MATHEW. 77 Full-Page Illustrations in Colour.

**The Italian Lakes**
Painted by ELLA DU CANE. Described by RICHARD BAGOT. 69 Full-Page Illustrations in Colour.

**Japan**
By MORTIMER MENPES. Transcribed by DOROTHY MENPES. 100 Full-Page Illustrations in Colour.

**Kashmir**
Described by SIR FRANCIS EDWARD YOUNGHUSBAND, K.C.I.E. Painted by MAJOR E. MOLYNEUX, D.S.O. 75 Full-Page Illustrations in Colour.

**Kent**
By W. TEIGNMOUTH SHORE. Painted by W. BISCOMBE GARDNER. 73 Full-Page Illustrations in Colour.

**Familiar London**
Painted by ROSE BARTON, A.R.W.S. 61 Full-Page Illustrations in Colour.

**London to the Nore**
Painted and Described by W. L. WYLLIE, R.A., and MARIAN AMY WYLLIE. 60 Full-Page Illustrations in Colour.

**London Vanished and Vanishing**
Painted and Described by PHILIP NORMAN, F.S.A. 75 Full-Page Illustrations in Colour.

**The Scenery of London**
Painted by HERBERT M. MARSHALL, R.W.S. Described by G. E. MITTON. 75 Full-Page Illustrations in Colour.

**George Morland**
By SIR WALTER GILBEY, Bt. 50 Full-Page Reproductions in Colour of the Artist's best work.

**Morocco**
Painted by A. S. FORREST. Described by S. L. BENSUSAN. 74 Full-Page Illustrations in Colour.

**Naples**
By AUGUSTINE FITZGERALD. Described by SYBIL FITZGERALD. 80 Full-Page Illustrations in Colour.

**The Royal Navy**
Painted by NORMAN WILKINSON. Described by H. LAWRENCE SWINBURNE. 61 Full-Page Illustrations in Colour.

**New Zealand**
Painted by the brothers F. and W. WRIGHT. Described by THE HON. W. P. REEVES, Lately High Commissioner for New Zealand. 75 Full-Page Illustrations in Colour.

**Norway**
Painted by NICO JUNGMAN. Text by BEATRIX JUNGMAN. 75 Full-Page Illustrations in Colour.

**Oxford**
Painted by JOHN FULLEYLOVE, R.I. Described by EDWARD THOMAS. 60 Full-Page Illustrations in Colour.

☞ PUBLISHED BY A. AND C. BLACK · SOHO SQUARE · LONDON · W.
AND OBTAINABLE THROUGH ANY BOOKSELLER AT HOME OR ABROAD

411

# BLACK'S BEAUTIFUL BOOKS

By Post, Price 20s. 6d.    THE **20s. NET** SERIES (*continued*)    Size 9×6¼ ins.

**John Pettie**
By Martin Hardie, B.A., A.R.E. 50 Full-Page Illustrations in Colour and 8 in Black and White.

**The Riviera**
Painted and Described by William Scott. 75 Full-Page Illustrations in Colour.

**Rome**
Painted by Alberto Pisa. Text by M. A. R. Tuker and Hope Malleson. 70 Full-Page Illustrations in Colour.

**Bonnie Scotland**
Painted by Sutton Palmer. Described by A. R. Hope Moncrieff. 75 Full-Page Illustrations in Colour.

**The Savage South Seas**
Painted by Norman H. Hardy. Described by E. Way Elkington, F.R.G.S. 68 Full-Page Illustrations in Colour.

**Northern Spain**
Painted and Described by Edgar T. A. Wigram. 75 Full-Page Illustrations in Colour.

**Southern Spain**
Painted by Trevor Haddon, R.B.A. Described by A. F. Calvert. 75 Full-Page Illustrations in Colour.

**Surrey**
Painted by Sutton Palmer. Described by A. R. Hope Moncrieff. 75 Full-Page Illustrations in Colour.

**Sussex**
Painted by Wilfrid Ball, R.E. 75 Full-Page Illustrations in Colour.

**Tibet**
Painted and Described by A. Henry Savage Landor. 75 Full-Page Illustrations in Colour.

**Venice**
By Mortimer Menpes. Text by Dorothy Menpes. 100 Full-Page Illustrations in Colour.

**Warwickshire**
Painted by Fred. Whitehead, R.B.A. Described by Clive Holland. 75 Full-Page Illustrations in Colour.

**Wessex**
Painted by Walter Tyndale. Described by Clive Holland. 75 Full-Page Illustrations in Colour.

**West Indies**
Painted by A. S. Forrest. Described by John Henderson. 74 Full-Page Illustrations in Colour.

**Yorkshire**
Painted and Described by Gordon Home. 71 Full-Page Illustrations in Colour.

By Post, Price 10s. 6d.    THE **10s. NET** SERIES    Size 9×6¼ ins.

**Bruges**
And West Flanders
Painted by A. Forestier. Described by G. W. T. Omond. 37 Full-Page Illustrations in Colour.

**The Light Side of Egypt**
Painted and Described by Lance Thackeray. 36 Illustrations in Colour, Cloth (album shape). Size 10½×8 ins.

**A Book of Porcelain**
Painted by William Gibb. Text by Bernard Rackham. 30 Full-Page Illustrations in Colour of Selected Examples in the Celebrated Collection of the Victoria and Albert Museum, London. (Size Crown Quarto).

**The Highlands and Islands of Scotland**
Painted by William Smith, Jun. Described by A. R. Hope Moncrieff. 40 Full-Page Illustrations in Colour

**From Sketch-Book and Diary**
By Lady Elizabeth Butler. 28 Full-Page Illustrations in Colour and 21 Line Drawings in the Text by Lady Butler.

By Post, Price 7s. 11d.    THE **7s. 6d. NET** SERIES    Size 9×6¼ ins.

**Abbotsford**
Painted by William Smith, Jun. Described by Rev. W. S. Crockett. 20 Full-Page Illustrations in Colour.

**Adventures among Pictures**
By C. Lewis Hind. 24 Full-Page Illustrations (8 in Colour and 16 in Black and White).

**Alpine Flowers and Gardens**
Painted and Described by G. Flemwell. 20 Full-Page Illustrations in Colour.

**The Beautiful Birthday Book**
By Gertrude Demain Hammond, R.I. 12 Full-Page Illustrations in Colour. Decorative Borders by A. A. Turbayne.

**Brabant & East Flanders**
Painted by A. Forestier. Text by G. W. T. Omond. 20 Full-Page Illustrations in Colour.

**British Floral Decoration**
By R. F. Felton, F.R.H.S., F.N.C.S., etc. (Florist to the late King Edward VII. and many Courts of Europe). 28 Full-Page Illustrations (12 in Colour).

**William Callow**
By H. M. Cundall, I.S.O., F.S.A. 22 Full-Page Illustrations in Colour and Numerous Illustrations in the Text.

**Canterbury**
By W. Teignmouth Shore. Painted by W. Biscombe Gardner. 20 Full-Page Illustrations in Colour.

**Chester**
Painted by E. Harrison Compton. Described by Francis Duckworth. 20 Full-Page Illustrations in Colour.

**A History of the Church of England**
By J. F. Kendall, M.A. Illustrated from Autochromes of the Church Pageant taken by Ernest C. Elliott. 24 Full-Page Illustrations (16 in Colour).

**Country Sketches for City Dwellers**
By Mrs. Willingham Rawnsley. 16 Full-Page Illustrations in Colour.

**Dutch Bulbs & Gardens**
Painted by Mima Nixon. Described by Una Silberrad & Sophie Lyall. 24 Full-Page Illustrations in Colour.

**Edinburgh**
Painted by John Fulleylove, R.I. Described by Rosaline Masson. 21 Full-Page Illustrations in Colour.

**English Costume**
Painted and Described by Dion Clayton Calthrop. In Four Sections, each containing 18 to 20 Full-Page Illustrations in Colour, and many Illustrations in the text: Section I. Early English—II. Middle Ages—III. Tudor and Stuart—IV. Georgian, etc. Price 7s. 6d. net each.

**Eton**
Painted by E. D. Brinton. Described by Christopher Stone. 24 Full-Page Illustrations in Colour.

**Eton from a Backwater** (Portfolio)
Painted by H. E. Luxmore. 12 Coloured Plates.

**Gardens of England**
Painted by Beatrice Parsons. Described by E. T. Cook. 20 Full-Page Illustrations in Colour.

**The Garden that I Love**
By Alfred Austin (*Poet Laureate*). Painted by George S. Elgood, R.I. 16 Full-Page Illustrations in Colour.

**The Charm of Gardens**
Text by Dion Clayton Calthrop. 32 Full-Page Illustrations in Colour (Size 9½×7 ins.).

**Geneva**
Painted by J. Hardwicke Lewis and May Hardwicke Lewis. Described by Francis Gribble. 20 Full-Page Illustrations in Colour.

**Grouse and Grouse Moors**
Painted by Charles Whymper, F.Z.S. Text by George Malcolm and Captain Aymer Maxwell. 16 Full-Page Illustrations in Colour (Size Large Crown 8vo.).

PUBLISHED BY A. AND C. BLACK · SOHO SQUARE · LONDON · W.
AND OBTAINABLE THROUGH ANY BOOKSELLER AT HOME OR ABROAD